Telegraph
The truth about
12-year-old boy our hope?
Sonny is
SONNY SCOR
CLEAR WINN
ONE Enfield youngster was having a ball last week when he secured a £3,000 sponsorship deal to help him on his way to a football career.
January 22-28 1996 No 165
70p
THE BIG ISSUE
Coming up from the streets
The next Ryan Giggs
40p of cover price goes to vendor
Soccer success proves catching
THE success of soccer sensation Sonny Pike seems to be inspiring other young hopefuls in the borough
Library to reopen
delayed
mercury sport — 5
Sonny outlook for a goalscoring sensation
Ajax net big catch in 11-year-old Cheshunt striker Pike
TOTTENHAM HOTS

THE GREATEST FOOTBALLER THAT NEVER WAS

Reach Sport

THE GREATEST FOOTBALLER THAT NEVER WAS

SONNY PIKE

WITH SETH BURKETT

For Freya and Beau

Reach Sport

www.reachsport.com

Published in Great Britain and Ireland in 2021 by
Reach Sport, a Reach PLC business,
5 St Paul's Square, Liverpool, L3 9SJ.

www.reachsport.com
@Reach_Sport

Reach Sport is a part of Reach PLC.
One Canada Square, Canary Wharf, London, E15 5AP.

Hardback ISBN: 978-1-911613-28-2
eBook ISBN: 978-1-911613-29-9

Photographic acknowledgements:
Sonny Pike personal collection, Reach PLC.
Every effort has been made to trace the copyright.
Any oversight will be rectified in future editions.

Design and production by Reach Sport.
Edited by Harri Aston.
Design: Lee Ashun. Production: Mike McGuinness.

Printed and bound by CPI Group (UK) Ltd,
Croydon, CR0 4YY.

Contents

Introduction: Enough

I walked around the pitch in a daze. The game took place all around me, the red and blue striped shirts of my Crystal Palace team-mates pushing back and forward against the white of Spurs. But not me. My body may have been on that pitch but my mind was a million miles away, my head all over the gaffe. What was I doing on that pitch, far out on the left wing where I always hated it? Who was I kidding?

From the outside I was a 14-year-old wonderkid with a world of possibility ahead of me. That's not how I saw it. I was still that worthless kid staring into the mirror. I was nothing. A joke. I looked down at the ground and wished it would open up and swallow me whole, golden Mizunos, curly barnet and all. At least that way I would no longer have to play football, to keep up with this whole charade. My head was ready to explode. The ball bounced nearby and despite my team-mates' calls I didn't even bother chasing it. What was I doing?

Nothing.

The words from my dad's explosive newspaper article still

rang in my ear. *Ex-wonderkid.* I closed my eyes and saw the yellow warning sign they'd printed over my face for the whole nation to ogle over. *Ex-wonderkid.*

Enough.

The game still happened around me, a long time left until the final whistle. That didn't matter. I'd made my decision. I couldn't do this anymore.

Nobody tried to stop me as I walked straight off the pitch. I walked and walked and didn't even make eye contact with any of my team-mates, nor with my stunned manager as I headed straight into the changing room,

When I closed the changing room door I was finally alone, just as I wanted.

After the game the manager, Martin Sprockett, tried to speak to me. He tried to put his arm around me and ask a few questions. It was pointless. No coach apart from Terry, who had always stood by me, had ever asked me how I felt, how all of the off-field stuff was affecting me, whether I was okay. Everything was always football related. I politely responded to all Martin said but didn't want to expand. He'd never understand. I didn't want to talk about football. I didn't want to do anything.

Nobody in that changing room knew what I'd gone through. To them, I was still Sonny Pike: Superstar. They didn't read the newspapers. They didn't know the chaotic home life. The civil war. The broken promises. In that changing room I stared at the floor as I heard my team-mates talking about the sad downfall of Pishu, playing for Spurs, that day's opponents, and also trying to rebuild his career after disaster. A shadow of what he used to be, I heard someone say. They might as well have been talking about me. I was finished.

At least they made it quick. At the very next training session I was called into a meeting with John Cartwright, the head of youth at Palace. My service was no longer required.

It was far from the first time I'd heard that.

From the promise of everything, I retreated into nothing. The paranoia returned, spurred on by the years of being in the media spotlight. Feelings of worthlessness grew. As the days became weeks and the weeks became months they nagged further, pushing me and pushing me closer to breaking point.

One day I found myself cycling back from central London with my mates, a rare respite from the stress and the strains of the constant rejections and disputes played out in front of the entire nation. We'd set off from Enfield early, planned to lose ourselves in the buzz. We went up and down the West End, around Covent Garden and China Town. People took no notice as we pedalled around, laughing and joking with one another. In those moments I felt happy, alive, normal.

It was only on the way home that those feelings changed. The 13 miles back home to Willow Road were miles where I was left to my own thoughts. I fully intended to stick with my mates, but as we approached Dartmouth Park Hill a new possibility occurred. Not only a new possibility. A new solution.

Everyone in Enfield knew the Archway Bridge. The place

that ended tens of lives a year, a mainstay of the Enfield Advertiser.

Man jumps off Archway Bridge.

Man dies falling from Archway Bridge

Calls for safety measures to be put in place at Archway Bridge

Locally, nobody called it Archway Bridge.

We called it Suicide Bridge.

I pedalled slower. My mates got further away. I knew there was a big downhill slope immediately after the bridge. Once they hit that, they would be gone.

I knew they wouldn't come back for me. They wouldn't think twice about waiting. I'd be alone.

At first it was the curiosity, but as I waited in a dusty little lay-by next to the bridge to make sure I was definitely alone, darker thoughts entered my mind.

I wondered what it would feel like, to feel nothing.

I dumped my bike and took a step toward the bridge. Then another step. I reached out and touched the bridge. The metal was cold. Putting my weight against the fence, I peered over. '1897' shone back at me in gold numbering, set against a dull red background. It's the date the bridge was built. So many years, so many lives.

If I looked up I'd have been able to make out St. Paul's Cathedral. I could probably have made out St. Bartholomew's Hospital, too, the place where it all started.

But I didn't look up, because all I could focus on was what was below. The cars rushing past. The unforgiving tarmac. The possibility.

The legs that were once insured for a million pounds began to shake. I thought of Dad, wondered if this was what he had in mind when he took out the policy.

You could do it.

The little voice in my head urged me on. I pictured myself jumping. I wasn't too high, but high enough for it to all be over in an instant. There wouldn't be any pain or suffering.

My hands remained glued to the fence, sweat seeping onto the cold metal. One movement. One chance to end it all.

It would be so easy.

It would end everything.

1: Sonny

I came into this world not as Sonny, but as Luke. Luke Santino Michael Victor Pike. But I've been known as Sonny ever since I can remember. It comes from my middle name, Santino. Just like Santino 'Sonny' Corleone in the *Godfather* films. As a boxing fanatic I reckon my father, Mickey, would also have been influenced by the fights of Sonny Liston, though I'm also sure that he fancied himself as a bit of a Don Corleone. Well, a Don Corelone who spent his time around building sites picking up odd jobs rather than co-ordinating his own crime network, but I suppose we can all dream.

My mum, Stephanie, was keen on the name too. She was trendy, always immaculately dressed in long trousers, a nice shirt, hair sticking up high at the front and sunglasses – always sunglasses – either perched on top of her stylish hair or down covering her eyes. Santino was stylish. It suited a lady of her style in the same way that it suited a boxing family like the Pikes. But the more they thought about it, the more they wondered whether there would be problems with the name later down the line. Would the kids at school laugh at someone with a funny name like Santino? They thought long and hard about it and ended up playing it safe with Luke. Fair enough, but I can count on one hand the number of people who have called me Luke over the years. There's something glamorous about Sonny. It draws people in. Has a ring to it.

My birth completed the Pike family. Dad finally had the boy he always wanted. Mum had her third child. And my two sisters – Dominique and Victoria, five and twelve years my senior – had the little brother they could fawn over. The five of us lived together in a flat above a fire station by Bow Flyover. Soon enough, though, we'd upped sticks to a flat in Hackney. No sooner had I settled then we were off again, to a bigger flat in Thornhill Square, Islington, two doors down from actor Michael Crawford and within walking distance of Arsenal's Highbury stadium. Money was tight and renting was expensive, but no matter where we moved to I always had family around. A lot of the extended family – my dad is one of nine siblings – lived in East London and I sometimes stayed for days at my grandparents' house in Hackney. Though it was only a two-up, two-down, it was always full of people, the doors always open to anybody who wanted to come in, and the parties were famous for lasting entire weekends, if not longer.

At those family gatherings there was invariably one topic on everyone's lips: boxing. Grandad Harry had previously run St. Monica's boxing club in Hoxton Square after his own fighting career, which included a draw on points against Charlie Kray. Following that, he became secretary at Repton for 12 years. He'd sit in a corner with my dad and Uncle Tim discussing up-and-coming fighters as the madness unfolded around them. The three of them used to call me over and hold up two cushions for me to spar against. Grandad Harry would get out his stopwatch and time me for a minute as I punched the cushions with all of my might.

"He can fight, Mick, he can fight! We'll get him down to Repton!"

"Yeah, but his mum doesn't want him to get bashed up," Dad would reply, a mixture of pride and disappointment evident.

There was a time when Dad was close to boxing professionally. Grandad Harry had always preached boxing and York Hall – the famous East London venue – quickly became their Mecca. Dad had all the attributes to make it: great, big hands, a stocky build, a presence on the canvas. He was only 5ft 10in but seemed to tower over his opponents. Power was his main asset – he could really pack a punch – and it was widely agreed that he had great potential. His short fuse and quick temper only enhanced those attributes. Grandad would work Dad into a rage and then he'd go out and destroy his opponent. In 20 fights at York Hall, Dad never lost one. Most of them were won by knockout. He was on the path to greatness. And then I came along.

Boxing. Fatherhood. In my father's mind, there was no way he could do both to the best of his ability. And so he gave up the boxing, vowing to never fight again. He'd sacrifice everything to focus on raising me.

After fighting the cushions at Nan and Grandad's I'd go next door to do my best Michael Jackson impression. Nanny Dolly took delight in playing his songs and one of my aunties made me a jacket with zips everywhere, just like the one MJ used to wear. Boxing was the warm-up; the MJ dance moves were the showpiece of every gathering.

We were always happy as a family. With Mum's mother, Nanny Vera, just down the road in Bethnal Green there were always people around. Nanny Vera in particular took delight in feeding me and spoiling me, though her house was a lot calmer. Nanny Vera had lost her husband back when my mum was just a teenager, and only a few years before that she'd also lost her daughter, Mum's sister Cheryl, to leukaemia. The dark times were long ago, but the whole family still felt their effects. Maybe that's why Nanny Vera made such a fuss of me and my sisters. Mum and Dad often spoilt us too. Dad's income as a builder wasn't regular and Mum was a full-time housewife, but they always ensured that us kids had plenty of love and attention. They'd take us on holiday once or twice a year and we had some really special trips, including one to Disney World in Florida. Victoria was still young enough to enjoy it and me and Dominique absolutely loved it, tearing around the theme park as the Donald Duck ears strapped to our heads swayed to and fro. As far as the Pike family was concerned, the East London years were the best of times.

And then everything changed. After years of renting, Mum and Dad decided to take the plunge and buy. I was due to start nursery in September and they wanted me to be settled. Only, I wasn't going to be settled in the familiar area of East London that I loved so much. There was no chance they could afford any of the places we'd been renting in so we ended up further north. They found a house in Enfield – still close enough to my extended family in East London but closer to Cheshunt, where Nanny Vera had just moved to.

Willow Road, Enfield. The house had potential. It was down a nice residential street of semi-detached houses, trees lining the road and a park just around the corner. There was a big metal spiral staircase leading up to three bedrooms: one for Mum and Dad, one for Victoria as the eldest sibling, one for me and Dominique to share. As with anything that has potential, though, it needed a bit of work on it first. Still, Dad was a builder and he was happy enough to take on the work himself. He hated working for free but he made an exception when it came to his own family. The estate agents seemed happy enough with the offer and my parents ended up getting the house for peanuts.

As a family we carried on where we left off. Each of us went off and did our own thing and sometimes we'd play a board game or watch TV together. I was always desperate to win anything we played and things could get quite lively, meaning we often ended up watching TV instead. Disney films were regulars with my sister, whereas my favourites became Live & Kicking, Fully Booked, Sister Sister, Fun House and Kenan & Kel. Often, we'd all be inside but by ourselves, doing our own thing. Mum and Dad did what they could to make sure we had nice things but life was different now. The house had been bought for peanuts but it still proved a financial strain. With Dad having to spend time not only doing the house up, but also building an extension to the back and side, paid work proved harder to come by. Whenever it did, Dad would then have to catch up with the work he was intending to do on the house in his own time. It was strenuous stuff. Physical labour is hard – really hard – and it takes its toll. Wears you down.

Dad had always preached hard work. Everything he did was influenced by the desire to graft and to set an example for his kids. He got us working too. Within weeks of moving into Willow Road, Dad had me heading out and knocking on the neighbours' doors with a bucket and mop, offering to wash their cars for cash. Dad had a get-up-and-go attitude, yet occasionally he must have looked back and wondered what could have been with the boxing. As the problems in Enfield grew, Dad found he no longer had boxing to channel his anger into. The fuse lit and there was nowhere to unleash his feelings. Nowhere except his own home.

They say opposites attract and Mum couldn't have been much more opposite. She was stylish; Dad was all about his jeans, white trainers and sports jackets. She preached karma, Dad was all about standing up for yourself. She was relaxed; Dad could never stop. She was calm; Dad was relentless. Opposites attract, but when the problems start, they repel each other.

As Dad's hard work wore him down more and more, as the strain of bringing up three children in a new area, of living on a building site, of never having enough money, become more prominent, their relationship became toxic. It wasn't long before the rows started. When I say rows, I really do mean rows. Great big massive full-blown rows which shook my insides. I'd have done anything to make them stop but, more often than not, I was dragged right into the middle of them. As the youngest I became a bargaining tool in their screaming matches. "He's going to live with me!" they'd scream. Instead of toning their anger down in my presence, I seemed to only add fuel to their fire.

The money problems became worse. The toxic rows became increasingly frequent. Dad got caught out with other women. Mum gave him a final chance, only to catch him out again.

Eventually, enough was enough. Our little family could no longer operate as a family.

Mum told Dad she wanted him out.

Nobody had ever stood up to Dad like that before. Nobody had ever told him he couldn't have his way.

We'd been in Enfield for a little under two years and it had already been too much for what had previously been a calm, loving family. Victoria was old enough for it to not really affect her when Dad moved out, but it hit me hard and Dominique, aged just 10, even harder. We longed for the old days of East London when my family was a tight unit – when I could walk to my nan and grandad's house or stay with my cousins. When we were together.

2: Changes

Life at home was becoming like a warped version of the hokey cokey. Mum and Dad were in, then Dad was out, then all of a sudden Dad was back in and Mum was out. And then Mum was back in and Dad was out. All the while me and my sisters were in, trying to lead a normal life and act like everything was fine.

Days were spent where I hoped and hoped that my family would get back together. I'd rack my brains for anything I could do to restore my tight family unit. There were moments when Mum and Dad were civil and my dreams appeared to become more realistic. But getting back together was never on the cards. The most toxic moments were hidden from me. Little did I know that Mum and Dad were well and truly at each other.

Money was the root of all of their problems. The separation had come about over money worries, and their warped hokey cokey then came about as they both attempted to claim rights to the house with what they each had in the bank. Dad came back in when he argued it was his money that bought the house. Mum moved to-Nanny Vera's in Cheshunt for a few months, then came back once she received council funding to help towards paying the mortgage on the house. Dad argued but his voice was less forceful than before. Deep down he knew that he couldn't afford to keep the house. But that wasn't all. He knew he didn't have it in him to act as both a mother and a father to me and my sisters. All of the work that my mum used to do – the cooking, cleaning, taking us to school – proved tough for him to manage alongside his day job. And so he moved out permanently.

Dad rented a little flat in a great, big tower block. One night, when I was staying over, we'd both been woken by a loud bang. Dad came into my room and told me everything was okay and to go back to sleep. The next morning, as we walked out of the block, there was a body-shaped section of grass that had been pushed down by the best part of a foot.

"Go over there and have a look," Dad said.

I was fascinated, but equally horrified. Dad told me to touch the ground and I reached out and prodded it with my finger. I couldn't get over how deep the ground had sunk. It was the resident on the ninth floor, Dad said. He was a teacher struggling with depression. Everything became too much and so he threw his TV through the window and then jumped down after it.

It wasn't long afterwards that Dad moved to a flat above an off-licence on Green Street, just a few roads from us on Willow Road, just over the other side of the A10.

With Dad close but not too close to Mum, everything calmed down. The two of them no longer had the energy to fight each other and even if they did, Dad knew that

Mum had won. He could beat her but he could never beat the council and the money they provided her with. And so they settled into their new way of life, even managing to become civil toward each other once again. They were able to have a conversation without breaking into a toxic row. The arguments were more or less a thing of the past. It helped that Mum pretty much did whatever Dad wanted. Even with the distance between us, Dad still maintained control over the family. He wasn't in the house most of the time but we always felt his presence. It was impossible not to. Dad had always been the leader of the pack. Without him the Pikes were broken. The family was broken.

It no longer felt like there was a family that lived in Willow Road. Instead there was a collection of people who loved each other, but they weren't a family. We never did anything together. There was no routine – not even a set mealtime. People just ate when they were hungry and fended for themselves.

Victoria spent most of her time up in her bedroom with her boyfriend Greg. He was as good as gold but the two of them needed their privacy. Dominique was more present but the most affected.

We'd still play-fight at night and she even managed to accidentally break my nose when a game we played in our bunk bed went wrong. In the game, the two of us would take turns to kick up from the bottom bunk, booting the person above up in the air. Once she caught me so well that I flew up in the air and on the way down my nose collided with the metal frame of the bed. Blood spurted up the walls as Mum ran in and grabbed my nose. After the doctor saw to it I had a new scar for life.

Weeks were spent with Mum in Willow Road and weekends were with Dad. Gradually, the home life of those first couple of Enfield years – disruptive, unpredictable and toxic – settled down, allowing me to enjoy far more the life that I lived away from home, which proved to be just as much fun, if not more so, than what I'd experienced in East London.

As soon as I was of age, Mum had enrolled me at the local primary school, Forty Hill. Everything about it seemed big, even though in reality it was small. The road it was on was quiet, the pupil numbers were just under 100 and the school itself was little more than a few connected buildings and a handful of portable cabins – more like an old style Victorian church than a school. To one side lay an actual church: Jesus Church Forty Hill, which had been an inspiration to our Church of England school since its beginnings in 1851. At the front was the playground which stretched the entire width of the school. And to the other side lay the playing fields: football pitch and all.

With single-form entry, class numbers rarely topped 15. Every morning the entire school would gather in the assembly hall to sing hymns and say the Lord's Prayer. The daily ritual was led by headteacher Mr Craig, who certainly seemed big, massive in fact – even bigger than the Year Sixes. He was a tall man who on first appearances looked intimidating and scary. The reality was anything but. Mr Craig was a gentle giant, his grey beard and bald head usually accompanied with a great smile. He made a point of learning all of the pupils' names and asking them about their interests. He was one of those people who could speak to anybody about anything. The example he set created a nice atmosphere where pupils could express themselves and enjoy their days at school.

I loved my days at Forty Hill. I didn't excel in the classrooms but school for me was never really about the lessons, though I did enjoy art – where I could let my mind wander – and wasn't too bad at maths. The less said about English the better. Concentrating for long periods of time proved problematic. Sitting still didn't interest me. Running about and laughing with my mates, though, was brilliant. I lived for break times, when we'd all play games like It and 1-2-3 Block Home. Mostly, though, we'd play football.

Coming from a boxing family, football had never really been on my radar before starting school. There was one exception, my mum's cousin Mark Falco, who was playing professional football for Queens Park Rangers after a lengthy period as a striker for Tottenham. He managed nearly 200 games for them and even won the UEFA Cup in 1984, but I never saw him that much and didn't really know of his achievements. I'd certainly never seen a game of football before starting school. Yet at break times I found the game of choice tended to involve jumpers for goalposts and, if we were lucky, a small foam ball. Usually, though, we'd have to play with a stone. Every lunchtime there'd be an elaborate search for the roundest stone possible. The pupils would then tear across the playground, knocking the roundish stone back and forth, dribbling it down the touchlines and then shooting into the goals marked either by jumpers, trees or on the playground wall depending on space. They say goalkeepers are mad and you had to be loopy to be a keeper for stone football.

Because everyone else played football, I started to play football. My closest mates at school were big fans. There was David Banfo, tall for his age and always scruffy. There'd often be half a sandwich down him but I would still grab him to celebrate when we scored goals on the playground. Richard Harvey, a Spurs fan and a keeper, meaning he was always useful; Stewart Edwards, an Arsenal fan and energetic player. The four of us regularly went round each other's houses, though it was David I was closest to, despite the fact he was in the school year above me. David carved out a real niche for himself as a commentator. On the playground every game was treated as if it were the FA Cup final, with David providing the excitable commentary as he played. He'd really nailed the Jim Rosenthal voice from the telly.

"And now it's John Barnes", he'd yell. "Barnes is on the ball. He's running down the wing. He goes past one, two, three defenders. They can't handle him! He looks up and sees Ian Rush in the middle." And there I'd be, in my customary position up front. The stone would roll over the concrete, never quite coming at me straight, and I'd watch it onto my black Kickers, guiding it between the two jumpers and past the helpless keeper. "And it's Ian Rush!" I'd yell, wheeling away in celebration, partly because that's what David did when he scored but also because it felt good to score. Especially when it won our team, Liverpool, the FA Cup.

Football in the playground came naturally to me. I soon spent a lot of my time playing the game. Lunch-time matches were competitive and captains always asked me to be on their team. Me and David proved inseparable though. There was absolutely no chance that Barnes and Rush could be split up.

Slowly but surely, football was taking a hold of me. I couldn't fight it and so I let it take me further and further, never realising that the sport was suffering from the same toxic atmosphere that I was experiencing in the life I had lived at home. I didn't know about hooliganism. I'd never heard of Heysel. I didn't know about the falling attendances, the dilapidated stadiums, the drinking, the riots, the racism. I barely even knew there was a whole world of football outside the high gates of Forty Hill. And even if I did understand what the sport was going through, I doubt it would have changed anything. You can't help what you fall in love with.

3: Cool Britannia

Football was a thing that I did and a thing I enjoyed. But in the summer of 1990, football became everything. The only thing. An obsession.

As the buzz of Italia 90 swept the school, the teachers took note. Those kids always kicking about on the playground: what if they were to kick around on an actual pitch with actual kit against actual opponents? And so it was that one morning, just after singing *Kumbaya My Lord* and just before repeating the Lord's Prayer, Mr Craig stood up at the front and as always happened when he did so, the pupils descended into a hush.

"It has been decided that Forty Hills primary school will have its first-ever football team," he said with his characteristic smile. "Mr Winch will be the manager. Players will be selected over the coming weeks for the school's first game against Lavender." There was pandemonium. Everyone was so excited. Finally! Our own team.

Lunchtime kickabouts gained a new level of intensity. Every game and every PE lesson became an opportunity to prove your ability. When the team was finally announced, many of the names were far from surprising. Chris Winch was Mr Winch's son, a rough, physical player who delighted in smashing into opponents. Stewart Gregory was capable of unleashing piledrivers, always whirring his arm round his body to wind up each shot. Whenever I saw that arm rotating I made sure to get out of the way. Albert Morris added quality to the team as a midfielder who could play a bit, getting the ball on the floor and passing it around. Lewis Davies was a winger who fancied himself as a bit tricky. And then there, the name right at the bottom, Sonny Pike.

I'd only just turned seven.

Chris Winch was nine.

Stewart Gregory was 11. All of the other players were in Year Five or Year Six. All except me.

It wasn't quite playing for England, but at the time it seemed to be the next best thing. I walked around the training pitch open-mouthed. The boys I lined up with for Forty Hill still seemed massive. I couldn't imagine what it was like to be that big. With some I could barely tell any difference between them and my teachers. Everything is big when you're seven.

My classmates had been buzzing about it all week. "Sonny's playing with the big kids!" they yelled.

I was just as excited. When the day finally arrived I pulled on the black and grey stripes of Forty Hill primary school, the kit still fresh from the manufacturers. And then I pulled on my school jumper. Mr Winch named me on the bench. I watched on from the sides as Chris Winch kicked our Lavender School opponents and Albert Morris sprayed the ball around. Mr Winch, a happy-go-lucky character, encouraged and encouraged. And then he told me to get warm.

I was sure I was going to be trampled on. The players were so big, the game so frantic. But as I stepped onto the pitch for the first time, all of my fears left me. It was just like being in the playground. I lost myself in the game, following the ball as it zipped around the pitch before positioning myself close to the opponent's goal. Then I waited. It wasn't long before the ball arrived and I reacted instinctively. The ball nestled in the net and the buzz was unreal. I'd scored a goal against the big kids!

From that moment on, I was in the school team. The goal earned me greater respect in the playground, as well as in the classroom. "Oh my God, Sonny is playing with the big kids!" they still yelled, though now with the addition of: "And he scored!"

Football was everything. I was no longer Sonny. I was Sonny the footballer.

David took it upon himself to educate me. I'd already sat in front of my TV in wonder over that long summer, watching the artistry of Beardsley and Platt and the sheer desire of Pearce and Butcher. Most of all, though, I watched Gazza. Under David's guidance I became a Liverpool fan, much to the horror of Stewart and Richard. I also began to watch their matches on TV, read about them in magazines, watch video tapes. It dawned on me that football was more than playground kickabouts. Football was a way of life.

More than that.

Football could be my life.

I was able to separate the thought of scoring goals in the playground and scoring goals for a living. As I immersed myself into this new world, the feeling became more and more concrete in my mind. I wanted to be a footballer when I grew up. I wanted it more than anything.

Lunchtimes, after school, weekends, everything became about football. The less I could be locked up inside a house, and the more I could be out on a pitch, the better. Recognising my new passion, Dad went out to get me my first ball. It was a red and white one with a picture of the official Italia 90 mascot, along with a Coca-Cola logo. I didn't let it out of my sight. I took it everywhere. With that ball I didn't even need team-mates to play against. I could just kick the ball by myself, pretending that I was taking part in the World Cup or scoring in the FA Cup final.

In the kitchen at Willow Road I used two cupboard doors as a goal, kicking my ball over and over again. Whenever I could I'd drag someone to go in goal. Mum was never that keen but my cousin Stefan was always willing to dive around the kitchen. Naturally, accidents happened. Cups and plates on the surfaces above the cupboards were frequently smashed. The chandeliers in the living room began to lose lights. Ball marks smattered the walls. It was no surprise when Mum encouraged me to spend more time over at the park.

Aldersbrook Park was literally across the road from Mum's house. Honestly, Mum could have thrown a stone from the kitchen and it would have hit me whilst I was playing there. Before long I was spending all of my time at

Aldersbrook Park. I'd turn left out of my house and knock for another park regular, Dan 'Bucky' Buck, who lived a few houses down. Though five years my senior, in Dominique's year at school, he proved to be a good mate and a reliable kickabout partner. Just around the corner on Aldersbrook Avenue lived a goalkeeper. Slightly further along, on the corner of Sandringham Close and right next to the entrance of the park, lived another goalkeeper, Tim. I was always after a goalkeeper to practise with and living so close to two left me feeling over the moon. I'd met both of them down the park and then clung onto them as close as possible, understanding just how useful they were. Anything to keep me from having to do my own shift in net.

If I knocked for both keepers I could guarantee that at least one would come out. Occasionally there'd be no answer at any of the houses. When that happened I'd just have to look down Sandringham Close, where I could usually find Lee Winkworth. He'd often be with a load of kids kicking around in the cul-de-sac.

"Hey, I'm going down the park now," I'd announce. "Come join me."

Usually, they all would. Italia 90 got a lot of people out into that cul-de-sac and down the park. Every single time I went through the entrance gates, I'd get so excited – even if I was by myself. I'd boot my ball as high in the air as I could then charge after it onto the grass. This was my Wembley. There was enough space for a single pitch, though there were no goals. There was no pitch marked either. Instead, it was a case of jumpers for goalposts or kicking against the fence.

The road and the play area were out of bounds. Everything else was fair game. If numbers were low then we would play sideways but most days we'd be playing 20-a-side. Strangers never put me off. If someone was kicking a ball around and I didn't know them, I'd ask to join in. It meant that I ended up playing with a whole variety of people of all ages. Proper matches, headers and volleys, Wembleys, re-enacting skills from the TV, football down the park never got boring. I could play all day and often I did. We never ate meals together as a family and I didn't have a time to be in. I'd usually skip breakfast so I could get down the park even earlier. If I felt hungry later in the day I'd then race back home, hopping the fence instead of taking the gates to save a precious few seconds. Most of the time I'd skip lunch as well and play the whole day until it got dark.

The kids in the park were even older than the ones I played with at school. Some of them were puffing and swigging before playing and yet I was getting picked before them when we split into teams. I was scoring more than them, too. I knew it meant I was all right. Each time I was picked to go on a team, I'd stroll out toward my captain, chest puffed out, and look at all the other kids who were still waiting to be selected. They were massive. They honestly looked like fully-grown men. Even the nine-year-olds seemed like they'd gone through puberty. And there I was, a seven-year-old kid not only playing in the same game as them, but being deemed better than them.

My new-found obsession hadn't been lost on Dad. He wanted to help me take my passion to the next stage and so he asked a few people for advice. They all pointed in the direction of Field End, the feeder team for Enfield Colts, the youth section of Enfield FC.

Dad took me over to Enfield playing fields for my first session with Field End. Right at the top of the playing fields was the Enfield FC stadium. Back then, they were a decent non-league team, having won the FA Trophy a couple of seasons earlier. They'd just been relegated to the Isthmian League after a number of strong years in the Football Conference, and at one stage it had even looked like the Football League could be a possibility. Games for Field End took place on the rest of the playing fields, which were like an Enfield version of Hackney Marshes. There must have been nearly 50 pitches of different shapes and sizes, all feeding up to the hallowed turf of the Enfield FC stadium.

They stuck me in goal for my first game. I'm not sure why and I paced about my goalmouth like a caged animal. From nowhere, a shot came my way. I dived and missed it. The ball nestled in the net and the other team tore away in celebration. I'd never felt disappointment like it. It was the worst feeling ever. Absolutely terrible. Gazza's tears multiplied by a million. "No, Sonny!" my new team-mates yelled. All I could do was stare back at them. I hadn't let the ball go in on purpose.

Why would anybody want to be a goalkeeper?

In the second half, they saw sense and put me up front. I took up my customary position in the other team's half and immediately started to make things happen. "Who's that girl, Dad?" a kid on the sidelines asked. "I don't know, son," came the response, "but nobody can get the bloody ball off her." My big curly hair bounced up and down as I weaved in and out of my opponents. I scored a goal, won the match, and from that moment on I was Field End's striker. Playing up front with Mario Lazaru, the son of manager Paul, the two of us started a healthy competition to see who could score the most goals. For about two games. It wasn't long before Mario's job became moving the ball on to me to make sure I could score the team's goals. Those were his dad's orders, and those were the screams of the watching parents. "Pass it to Sonny!"

Field End was a great team to develop with. Paul Lazaru was a typical dad running a football team. There were no airs and graces about him. He wasn't the kind of manager to overload his players with information and trial new formations. He just gave us a ball and off we went. Everything was low key. He wanted us to enjoy playing with a smile on our faces, and he made sure he always coached with a smile on his own. In our sky blue and white striped kit, just like Argentina, we swept aside teams.

A new ritual developed. Football becoming something that me and Dad did together. Our way of bonding. Dad would come over to Mum's house on Willow Road every Saturday morning and take me on the short walk to Enfield playing fields. There, we'd meet the other boys and their parents at the football stadium, next to the posh club at the side of the bar called the Starlight Rooms. Sometimes we'd meet inside the Starlight Rooms and ogle at the football memorabilia inside. There were posters and pendants and a great big picture of the victorious Enfield side at Wembley, ex-Spurs player Steve King grinning at the front. I spent hours staring at that picture. Wembley. Enfield had played at Wembley. Enfield had won at Wembley. If that Enfield lot had gone to Wembley then why couldn't I go to Wembley? I was an Enfield player, too. Maybe I could do that. The thought of it filled me with sheer excitement.

From the Starlight Rooms, we'd go to our game before returning to the football stadium to celebrate our victory or forget our loss. Usually, it was to celebrate. Us kids would play games of pool while the dads stood around the edge of the room, beer in hand. Every now and again, we'd break from the games to sprint out onto the first-team pitch, kicking a ball for as long as we could until the inevitable call came from the grumpy old groundsman. "Oi!", he'd scream. "Get those bloody kids off there." It never failed to make us laugh. The rest of the day would be spent playing football on and off before it was back to Dad's to watch the football highlights. On Sundays I'd be off to Aldersbrook Park, my red and white ball tucked under my arm and at least one goalkeeper by my side, ideally two.

Dad came to every one of my games, whether it was for Field End or the school team. Sometimes he'd be on the sideline, other times he'd be watching from his car, but he was always there. He didn't know the first thing about football – his whole life had been boxing, boxing, boxing – and if you saw him attempt to kick a ball you'd probably laugh. He couldn't tell the difference between a sweeper and a No10, but he enjoyed spending time with me and encouraging me in something I loved doing. That was fine with me.

Every now and again, Dad would give me an extra bit of motivation to play well. "Here, Sonny. If you score a hat-trick today I'll buy you a new pair of boots," he'd wink at me. That was always the best incentive. Usually it'd be money, but occasionally it'd be new boots. Dad soon realised his motivations always worked. If he asked me to score a goal I'd score. If he encouraged me to score five, I'd score five. I must have been horrible as a team-mate because I didn't really care whether my team won or lost – only that I played well and scored lots of goals. I must have been even worse as a strike partner because there'd be times when all I could think about was Dad's bet. There was no chance of me passing the ball.

Dad often joked that I was going to clear him out of house and home, though given our money troubles it may not have been too far from the truth. It was his own fault though. He was so good at getting me geed up for games. He didn't know football so he relied on what he did know: boxing. Dad knew how to get me focused before a game. He took my easygoing nature and made me into a warrior on matchday. "Look", he'd say to me before games, "I'll take you to this game but you gotta take it seriously. There's a difference between winning and coming second." It was always about first and second. After those talks I never wanted to lose in my whole life. Winning was everything. "But Sonny", he'd go. "You don't need to worry about anyone else. You just gotta go on the pitch and do your work. The only person against you is yourself. If you do your best you'll be fine. But if you don't then it's just not gonna work. Only your best is good enough."

I'd charge onto that pitch absolutely desperate to win. I'd have done anything to impress my dad. Every kid's hero is their dad and I wanted to impress mine more than anyone else. The competitive mindset he instilled in me from boxing gave me an edge over the other kids. He'd watch fights with me and give me an insight into the boxers. One particular bout sticks in my memory, the 1989 fight between Mike Tyson and Frank Bruno. I was just five years old and crept into the living room in the middle of the night to watch from behind the sofa. Dad spotted me, but instead of sending me back to bed he got me up on his lap next to Uncle Victor. The two fighters walked out and, even thousands of miles away from the safety of the sofa, I could feel the atmosphere in the venue. It was truly electric. For Tyson especially – the 'baddest man on the planet' – the crowd went wild.

"Who's going to win?" I asked Dad as the fighters sized each other up before touching gloves. I was thinking it would be Bruno, who was so much bigger than Tyson. He was looking at Tyson and Tyson was staring back. There was something in that stare.

"Bruno's lost this fight already," Dad replied. He went on to tell how Tyson's mental drive was on a whole different level to Bruno's. Bruno was looking at Tyson, acting tough, but it was just an act. For Tyson, the look came from something deep within him. A desire to win.

Dad introduced me to the mental side of sport and then fostered that desire in me. I watched on as Tyson won, and then Dad watched on as he led me through pad work, using the cushions as a punchbag. That was at five years old and, when I started playing football, that desire and intensity was applied just the same. But sometimes it used to drive me mad. I'd get so wound up on the pitch that I'd roar if I made a mistake. If I missed an easy chance I'd hit myself. I'd literally be stood there in the opposition's area, a seven-year-old kid, slapping and pinching his legs and screaming in a ridiculous mix of anger and regret.

With a mindset like that, I was gutted whenever I let Dad down. After losing a cup final I refused to pick up my runners-up medal. When it's drilled into you that you've got to come first, coming in second place hurts. On the rare occasions that I didn't score in a game, I'd be desperate to play the next one and put everything right. Whenever that happened, Dad's words hurt far more than anything I could have done to myself. "You were fucking shit today, son," he'd tell me as I got into the car, his eyes straight ahead on the road. Tears would well up in my eyes but I didn't want to let Dad see me crying.

The solution for both of us was to train even harder. I'd be down the park, working late into the night and Dad would often join me, throwing the ball in the air for me to volley against the fence with either foot. Sometimes I'd mishit my volleys and Dad would grab me by the scruff of the neck, rocking me back and forth. Ragdolling, it's called, because when you're shaken like that you appear as limp as a ragdoll. Dad would regularly do it to me if I wasn't concentrating or if I did something stupid, yelling at me to "sort yourself out". It became normal. I knew Dad was quick tempered and I knew he loved me and was doing it out of the goodness of his heart.

I had a few more bruises than before from hitting myself in anger but it was a small price to pay for the success I was having on the pitch. Soon enough, with 49 goals I'd established myself as the top goalscorer not only for Field End, but in all of the Enfield leagues. With my technique I was able to kick the ball further than pretty much every other kid my age, and because we played on full-sized pitches with full-sized goals, I knew I could always place the ball above the goalkeeper. As the goals racked up, people started to take note. I was getting into the local paper and even making a couple of headlines. After my first season with Field End, our team became Enfield Colts. I was already well known by people across the league. And even beyond. A few weeks after my eighth birthday, I got into the car with Dad after a game and he told me that he'd been approached after one match by a man in a Tottenham Hotspur jacket.

A scout.

The scout wanted me to train with the youth academy of Tottenham.

"What do you think, son?" Dad asked me.

I shrugged, said I didn't know, I wasn't really too bothered. I'd already decided I was going to play for Liverpool. Tottenham wasn't Liverpool and so it didn't seem like it would make too much difference whether I played for Enfield or Tottenham. Either way, it wasn't Liverpool.

The offer hung over both of us. It was on open invitation and Dad had the scout's number written down back at his house. "Well then," he announced one afternoon after school when we were sitting together in McDonald's. "It's Thursday and there's that Tottenham training this evening. Do you want to go?" I scooped up a chicken nugget and dunked it into my pot of sweet and sour sauce. I didn't really want to go. I shook my head.

"Okay, son. Don't worry about Tottenham", he said, his arm draped around me. "We've got plenty of time to get where we need to be. We'll see what happens."

And Dad was right. There was no rush. We had no need to push too far. With Dad's boxing mindset, patience was seen as a virtue. You carry on attacking your opponent, focusing on your own ability, ignoring your own weaknesses, and waiting for greatness to come.

4: Making a Name

SONNY SCORES A CLEAR WINNER

My name wasn't unfamiliar to the *Enfield Independent* but this was different. This was a whole article dedicated just to me, with a great big picture of my face staring out from the print.

And most importantly of all, it told how a local company, Home County Windows, had agreed to pay £3,000 to help me with my ambition to become a professional footballer. They'd heard all about my potential. They'd seen that I'd scored 11 goals in a single game. Mainly, though, they'd heard that Spurs had been interested but I wanted to play a more European style.

I don't remember saying that but I certainly wasn't complaining about the money. I went straight down to Goodman Sports, a shop in Chase Side, Southgate, and ordered a load of training kit. It was unbelievable.

The kids at school all saw the article and word quickly spread, yet to me everything seemed normal. Over time, as my goalscoring exploits continued to attract attention, it would become even more normal to be featured. The headlines came naturally.

SONNY'S GOALS LEAD COLTS TO VICTORY

ANOTHER FINE PERFORMANCE FROM SONNY

It wasn't just the local newspaper that was suddenly attracted to football. The trend was national. Something called the Premier League had just started up. Twenty teams broke away from the English Football League to form their own all-singing, all-dancing league covered by Sky Sports. It was impossible to escape the noise. More column inches were filled, with football given great coverage than ever before.

And as a result, football was getting richer.

Players were becoming more than just footballers. Instead, they were entertainers.

It suited me. Football had truly become my life. I gobbled up anything to do with the sport that I could get my hands on. After getting my first ball, Dad bought me a video tape that featured the skills of Johan Cruyff, Diego Maradona and Pele. I was transfixed. Again and again I played the tape, my face inches from the screen. Then I'd rush outside and try to copy the skills I saw. When it got too dark to train I'd return home and then play the tape again, watching Pele doing keepie-ups with a coconut, Maradona slaloming between opponents and Cruyff doing his iconic skill. Mum used to do her nut in when her soap operas were scheduled to come on TV and I was still watching my video tape.

Sometimes Dad would watch it with me, and eventually

he learned what each skill was called. Back then, football in England was very direct. There was a lot of route-one play going on, hitting the ball into the channels and competing to win flick-ons. Skills were looked down on as something that foreigners did. But I was desperate to try and copy what I saw on my video tape. Dad helped by writing the skills on the inside of my fingers before games. When the whistle blew, I'd look down at my hands and decide which skill I'd try to use next.

"You look like a ballerina with those skills," Grandad Harry used to laugh. He wasn't the only one. I'd try my skills at the park and kids would wonder what I was doing. Then I'd tell those same kids about Cruyff, Pele and Maradona, and Boca Juniors, Santos and Ajax, and they'd look at me like I was from a different planet. Back then information wasn't readily available on the internet and because I wanted to know everything I could about Cruyff, Maradona and Pele, I spent my time scouring books, magazines and video tapes for anything to do with football. Whenever football was on I'd watch it. It didn't matter if it was England or Enfield. The more different, the more I found myself attracted to it.

Whenever I had the chance, I'd play. It didn't matter if the kids were younger than me or 10 years older, whether I was in Enfield or Edmonton or over in Hackney, if I had the chance I'd play. If it wasn't street rules it'd generally be structured matches with Enfield.

Dad got me involved with the age group above at Enfield Colts. His mate Jimmy Hoskins ran the team and I began to train with them along with another player my age, a keeper called Adam whose own father was also mates with Jimmy – so much so that Adam referred to him as 'uncle', while everyone referred to Adam as 'hitman'. Naturally, the two of us stayed close together but we more than held our own, emerging as two of the best players. And then I came across Terry.

Everyone in Enfield knew Terry. He was the man who went up and down the park on his bike watching as many games as he could. Rumour had it that he coached a team in each league. No matter how accurate that rumour was, every team Terry coached won. There was Pacific Athletic. Pathetic Athletic, Terry had called them, when he first coached them. Under his guidance they went from the bottom of the Edmonton 10th division to the top of the first. He was most well-known, though, for his work with Foxes Youth, the all-conquering local team – featuring future Watford and Chelsea striker Paul Furlong – that had almost taken over Germany but for a narrow 1-0 defeat against a south German representative side.

If you were any good and played around Enfield, Terry knew about you. And not long after I started playing for Enfield, Terry knew about me. At first he'd be on the sidelines, perched on his bicycle and taking in the game. Then he started congratulating me. "You all right, boy?" Terry would ask of me as I walked off the pitch. "Well played." I'd always nod back at the ex-army trainer in his 50s, small in stature but lean and fit as a butcher's dog. As time went by, I could usually count on him to be alongside Dad at each of my games.

But Terry didn't just watch games and coach his own teams. He'd also set up open sessions for anyone who wanted to take part. It was free to take part. There was just one rule: every participant had to have their own ball. Kids would finish their matches and then head over to the small square patch of grass Terry marked out by Southbury Road eager to learn. "A ball, a ball, a ball," Terry would repeat over and over. Everything had to be done with the ball. Even on the rare occasions he'd ask us to run round the fields, he'd ask: "Why don't you take your ball with ya?"

Nobody else coached like that.

For all other coaches, grassroots football was about the three basics: kick, bollock, bite.

They wanted players to go flying into tackles, run their bollocks off and be nasty. But not Terry. He'd been heavily influenced by his time spent in Germany. He'd played in their leagues for SC Paderborn, who'd go on many years later to play in the Bundesliga. After playing, he did his coaching badges over there, learned their methods and then put them into practice back in England. For Terry, grassroots football was all about the ball. He couldn't stand kick, bollock, bite, even less so than cheats. "Play the game or you're out!" he'd yell in the training matches he put us in.

The more I watched my tapes of football overseas, the more I learned the style of football that Terry had experienced, the more alluring football abroad seemed. And then I had the chance to experience the world of Cruyff for myself. Enfield FC were taking part in a football tournament at the end of the season. All players were invited, and because we were only nine years old our parents were too. We would be going all the way to Holland to play against teams from all over Europe.

I couldn't have been more excited.

A whole holiday where all I'd do was play football.

I hadn't been on a holiday abroad since Mum and Dad split up.

And I'd never been on a holiday where all I did was play football.

The video tape took on a new meaning. I watched the Johan Cruyff segments religiously, imagining playing against his mini descendants and standing out as the best player on the pitch. Even Dad did a bit of research. He hadn't hesitated when he heard about the tournament, agreeing to come along in an instant. He'd find the money, don't worry about that.

Dad told me all about Coerver coaching. Apparently it underpinned all of the youth development of Dutch players, prioritising ball work to create highly technical footballers. It sounded just like the kind of training Terry preached.

I counted down the time to my football holiday, getting even more excited with each passing day. It didn't matter that I'd never heard of Den Haag, where the tournament was taking place. It didn't matter that I'd never heard of ADO Den Haag, the tournament hosts. All that mattered was that I was going to the country of Cruyff, of Ajax, and if ADO Den Haag and the other teams were anything like Ajax then I'd be in a special place.

After what felt like an eternity, the day arrived. I kissed my mum goodbye, waved to my sisters and looked at my house one last time before heading off to meet my Enfield team-mates in Dad's white van. They were all just as excited as me. A holiday! To play football! From the port at Dover, we set sail on our first-ever football holiday, my first-ever trip to Europe. It was exciting enough to get out of North London, let alone England.

When we pitched up for our first game of the tournament, however, I started to wonder what all the hype was about. There didn't really seem to be any difference in the style of football. We were only a stone's throw from Rotterdam, where Dutch giants Feyenoord were based, but the teams appeared to be no different from those I played against every week in England. There was no superiority. No total football. No outlandish skills. The football was maybe played at a quicker tempo, though the fact we were competing in an international tournament would have helped that. Everyone was desperate to win, myself included. I had shown the teams around north London what I could do and now it was time to prove myself to Europe.

On a personal level, I did well. The goals, as they always seemed to back then, flowed with ease. Hearing the swish of the net as my shots nestled was just as satisfying as it was back in Enfield, and the defences proved just as accommodating. Unfortunately, our team didn't play to its full potential. We won a couple of our games but it wasn't enough to see us through to the final.

Even so, we loved it. The weather was great, the games were a fantastic experience and the supporters were passionate. I must admit that up until that first game I was wondering who on earth ADO Den Haag were, but their passionate supporters cheering on the boys in green and yellow soon gave me a new-found respect for them.

Our parents also seemed to enjoy the tournament. It was a chance for them to let their hair down and, to an extent, pass on their responsibilities for us to our coach. I say to an extent, because even though it was the coach's task to make sure we were safe whilst the tournament was on, our parents still had to oversee us when we were back at our hotel.

For my father it was a bit of a test. Him and Mum were really traditional in their methods. They believed that it was the man's job to provide for the family, to be the breadwinner, and the woman's job to raise the children. When Dad moved out it meant he had to take a bit more responsibility – when we visited him he couldn't just get Mum to help with any menial parenthood that was required as she wasn't there – but he still wasn't really doing the day-to-day stuff that a mother, especially a single mother, traditionally does.

I don't know if that meant he felt under more pressure whilst in Den Haag. It was the first time I'd ever been away with him. Even back in Enfield I'd rarely spend extended time with just Dad beyond football. If it was a day out there'd usually be my sister, Dominique, there. It always made our excursions a little less full-on. And now here I was, suddenly thrust together with him in a small chalet. We had a chalet to ourselves, as did every other parent and child combination. To be honest, I was pretty chuffed. What young boy doesn't idolise his father? Though most of the time was spent either at the tournament, travelling, or with the rest of the team in the communal areas, it still meant we had a lot of time together. I cherished those moments with him. He didn't really understand much about the games we played in, but it didn't take an expert to realise when I scored a goal. Each night he'd talk with excitement about what lay ahead on my path to greatness. He was enthused by what he saw on the pitch, and it only motivated me further.

It was a nice mix: football in the day, quality time with Dad in the evening and plenty of larking about with friends in between. The complex we were staying at was pretty tailored to groups such as ours. With facilities aplenty it gave our childhood imaginations a chance to run wild. There was a big wooden hut in the centre where all the parents and players would congregate for meals. It also gave the parents a base where they could happily sit and socialise while we went off out into the wild. The hut was big enough to see from all parts of the complex so there was no danger of any of us getting lost.

Or so I thought, because the penultimate night of the tournament changed everything. With the day's games over I was out playing on the gravel behind the hut with a couple of team-mates, blissfully unaware that Dad was trying to find me. As team-mates and parents headed in the direction of the communal area, we decided to join them for what we presumed would be dinner. I turned the corner and there he was, seething. He was really mad. It had been no longer than five minutes since I'd last caught a glimpse of Dad but that didn't matter. His fists were contorted, his face reddening with every second. His words came out and he screamed them at me, effing and blinding so angrily that he stopped me dead in my tracks.

"Where the fuck was ya?" he bellowed.

I'd done nothing wrong. I knew it, but I still surprised myself as my mouth opened to protest my innocence.

"I was just with my mates."

The next few seconds were a blur. I was upright, staring defensively at my dad and then I was down and out for the count. Those six words were the final straw. My mouth had barely closed when Dad sprung forward. For years after I could still vividly hear the sharp clunk of the gravel as his leg sprung into action. In one swift motion he grabbed my head with one hand, slamming it down against his uprising knee. He was a powerful man, my dad, and as a nine-year-old boy I didn't stand a chance. Down I went, everything black.

Over the next few minutes I slipped in and out of consciousness, not really registering what was happening to me. A crumpled heap on the unforgiving gravel, Dad pulled me up by the armpits. I couldn't resist. He was too strong for me and I didn't have any energy to fight him anyway. All I could do was accept my fate. Dad dragged me along to the wooden hut, my legs jelly, and plonked me down on a bench. I had to concentrate so hard to make every single step. The next thing I knew there was a plate of food in front of me. It was horrible. I'm a fussy eater at the best of times but what greeted me was enough to shake me back into unconsciousness. I really, really didn't want to eat it. I didn't want to look at it. But who was sitting opposite me? He'd done it on purpose, even in my state at the time I knew that. He'd picked a meal he knew I hated and given me no other option. What else could I do? After what had just happened there was no chance I could refuse to eat it. I was absolutely terrified of what would happen if I didn't.

It felt like hours, but eventually I managed to force my way through most of that plate. Still in a daze, I excused myself and headed back to the chalet. Dad was still at the table, chatting away. He had this amazing knack of being overly nice to people, especially when the situation demanded it. When he was nice he really was nice. But there was a darker side to him. His temper was short and when the fuse was lit, well, it was best to be a long way away from him. This wasn't like the ragdolling back in Enfield. This was something far more serious. Terrifying.

5: Goal Machine

As a kid your dad always seems powerful. He's your role model, the epitome of masculinity, and so you're always a bit fearful of getting a clip round the ear from him. What happened in Den Haag made me realise what my old man was truly capable of, however. What was a clip round the ear when I could be on the receiving end of one of his right-handers? How could I ever disobey or displease him again, if that was what was going to happen? The alternative was too disturbing to contemplate.

That trip to Holland was the end of our progression with Enfield FC. The team disbanded, players moving on to all kinds of clubs in the local area. I ended up at Charlden Youth, kicking on from where I left off. Dad was at my side as always, his presence as powerful as ever. I fell into line, always doing either as he wanted or as I thought he wanted. Which wasn't always the worst thing in the world. Dad especially knew how to push my buttons and get me buzzing before a match, which gave me a mental edge over the other kids. Just before the warm-up, he'd get down on one knee and I'd put my right boot on top of his blue jeans. I'd lace it up and then wrap the laces twice around the boot, pulling the tongue down as far down as it would go. I always liked my boots as tight as possible. Dad learned not to worry about the circulation in my feet. I'd give him one last look and think, even given that moment in Den Haag and the ragdolling and the constant control, we had an amazing partnership going. What he did, he did out love. It was the two of us, him totally out of his comfort zone in a sport he didn't know anything about, trying his best to make me a star, me improving with every game. Dad would then get me to flick a pretend switch on my leg and with that I was transformed from mere Sonny Pike into Sonny the goal machine.

It worked.

That first season with my new club I managed to score 120 goals, as well as get called up to the Harlow league representative team. Our first season finished with victory in a cup final, played at non-league side Sawbridgeworth Town in a proper stadium and with my dog Winston as mascot! Even Mum came along to that game, watching on as we added the cup to our league title. People took notice of our success. The columns became bigger. More journalists started reporting on the boy wonder.

And soon I wasn't the only member of the Pike family they were reporting on. As my status in football was rising, Dominique's reputation as an actress catapulted when she was cast in the upcoming series of Grange Hill, a BBC drama portraying life in a secondary school. She was to play Madelaine, a new girl at the school who joined the girls' football team as they trained for a showdown game against the boys. We were all so excited for her, thinking this would be her first step to becoming a major actress. Soon after the news, a big article appeared in the local paper with a leading image of her in the red Grange Hill jumper throwing a ball up into the air, her eyes trained on it. Months later, her first episode aired. We all gathered together in the living room – even Dad – ready for her big introduction. And then there she was, walking down the school corridor in the iconic red jumper. 'Wow' I thought as I looked between the Dominique in my living room and the Dominique on TV. It's really her – my sister – on national television. True to character, she soon got into an argument with one of the other characters. 'Go on!' we shouted. More episodes followed, all of them leading up to the big match. The boys of Grange Hill thought they'd all have it their way, but the girls gave them a good game. That was until Dominique scored the own goal that lost them the match. It was her final act. After Grange Hill she got a job as a runner on Red Dwarf, another step closer to realising her dream.

With our upward trajectories, as well as our oldest sister, Victoria, doing well on her script supervisors' course at the Anna Scher drama school on Copenhagen Street, it was a brilliant time for the Pikes. And it only became more brilliant when the television crews moved from Dominique to me.

London Tonight was the first television crew to get in touch. They'd read all about my heroics in the *Enfield Advertiser* and *Independent*. They'd seen the article that detailed the 11 goals I scored in one game for Charlden

Youth against a team called Jaguar. I'd got a little lucky in that match because the pitch we were playing on had a slope and we were kicking downhill in the first half. In every game I played, I looked to score a hat-trick. Dad would always tell me to aim to score three, and if Dad told me to do it then I was certainly going to. In that match, aided by the slope, I skipped off at half-time with the double hat-trick very much a possibility. I'd scored five goals. There was no chance I was letting up there. I scored early for the double hat-trick, then got my treble hat-trick. The goals came easily. Back then teams played on full-sized pitches with full-sized goals. Keepers could barely reach the edge of their areas with goal kicks, meaning strikers could just lay in wait like true predators. I'd get the ball off goal kicks, dribble past one player and then lift it high into the net where the keeper couldn't reach it. Ten goals. Eleven goals. And then, cruelly, the final whistle blew before I could complete my quadruple hat-trick.

After that, everyone was talking about me.

Including the producers at *London Tonight*.

At my next match, we were greeted by a film crew. Dad drove me and my mates over to the game as always. They used to love those car journeys. There were no seatbelts, always a couple of us lying in the boot and Dad doing his best to throw us about all over the place while blasting Chas & Dave at full volume. "Look at what he's doing now!" they'd scream with joy. Me and Bucky became massive fans of Chas & Dave as a result of those car journeys. But as we stepped out of the car we found that the camera crew had nothing to film. The game, due to take place just over the other side of the A10 at Bush Hill Park, had been cancelled just an hour before the kick-off. Some of our opponents had made the trip unaware, however, and between them and those watching on the sidelines, plus our substitutes, we had just about enough for a full game. Bucky ended up in goal for the other team. That wasn't ideal because not only was he a decent footballer, but he was five years older than me. I could hardly just lob him like most of the keepers my age. He could touch the crossbar, for a start.

Walking out in the Dutch-style orange top, black shorts and black socks of Charlden. I had my own personal cameraman. They insisted on filming me lacing up my pride and joys: my bright yellow Quasar boots. Whatever was about to happen, in those boots I always knew I'd stand out.

Dad was joined on the sidelines by my mum and sisters, as well as Nanny Vera. That's how I knew it was a big occasion. Nanny Vera had never come to watch a match before. "Good luck, son!" she yelled. 'What the hell is she doing here?' I wondered, waving back sheepishly. "Go on, son!" Mum added, my sisters and Dad smiling next to her like the perfect happy family.

Any feelings of nervousness disappeared as soon as the game started. I could always lose myself in football, forget whatever was happening around me. Soon enough I scored my first goal. I picked up the ball on the edge of the box, went round a couple of defenders and drew Bucky out of goal. I faked to shoot and then went round him as well before rolling the ball into the empty net. As I turned to celebrate I felt a new presence at my side. The cameraman had run on to the pitch to get a close-up of my celebration!

Woah. What's going on here?

Twice more I peeled off to celebrate goals. Twice more the cameraman ran onto the pitch. At the end of it all we had won 3-1 and I had scored all three goals. The game couldn't have gone any better.

Afterwards, I was asked a series of questions about my football and my inspirations. With football no longer there to distract me, the nerves came back and I stumbled over a couple of lines. The interviewer seemed happy enough though and a few days later the Pikes once again gathered together in the living room for the latest television appearance.

'We're gonna make you a star' the speakers blared out the 1975 hit by David Essex. 'We're gonna make you a star. He is so much more than a pretty face.'

And then there was my face, right there on the TV.

"Sonny Pike, the boy with the golden boots..." the newsreader announced as footage of me in action played on the screen. Bloody hell, I thought as I watched the images, is this really happening? This isn't normal. All of my team-mates were there and yet the entire focus was on me, the whole segment dedicated to the kid with curly hair. This was no longer local. Everything had gone up a level.

My mates down the park were buzzing. They were so happy for me and had all seen the segment. At school, Mr Craig was so pleased. Mrs Moore, my teacher, told all of my classmates about the piece. She'd always given me preferable treatment because of my football, and whenever she called me up to the front of the class to read she'd ask if I had a football book for her. I always did. As I read and got toward the inevitable crescendo when the wonderkid scored a goal, she would gasp and exclaim "just like you do!" with a big smile.

The 'wonderkid' title was becoming harder to escape.

More film crews followed. Sky Sports invited my mum's cousin Mark Falco down to a game for Charlden. As part of the segment he gave me some advice from his time in the game, having recently retired after two seasons with Millwall. "Just concentrate," he told me for the cameras. "Do your thing." Some came down to the school gates, where instead of Mum's bright yellow Suzuki Jeep I'd be greeted by Dad and a load of cameras. "Come on," he'd beckon to me and I'd run into his arms for a hug. It didn't take me long to realise how important giving off appearances was for the camera. Other crews went with filming me playing and then interviewing me afterwards. In each of the clips they told of this boy wonder who was surely the next big thing. They asked for my inspirations and I told them about the video tape with Cruyff, Maradona and Pele.

Cruyff. It always came back to Cruyff. And when the *Enfield Independent* added a quote from my dad about my desire to play in Holland, the Dutch Embassy took note. They sent the footage and the article across the water to a Dutch production company who watched with interest. A curly-haired English kid talking about his love of a Dutch legend? In their eyes it made for a great story. Later that week they were in England, standing on a freezing cold touchline in deepest Harlow, a set of cameras pointed in my direction as I dribbled past opponents this way and that.

As soon as the game finished they grabbed hold of me. Filming the match was only a small part of what they were after. First they wanted to ask all about Cruyff. I repeated my lines about the video tape and about how much football abroad appealed to me. There was more they wanted, though. They drove back to my mum's house on Willow Road, following behind Dad who led the way, and once there they wanted me to show them round my bedroom. I led them upstairs and showed them my football books and videos, then pointed to the posters on the walls, which were pretty much a 50/50 split between Liverpool and players from abroad. There was Cruyff, of course, but also Bryan Roy, Dennis Bergkamp, Jamie Redknapp and Ian Rush.

"Can you just pretend to sleep on your bed for a minute?" the cameraman asked me. Pretend to sleep? It was 2 o'clock in the afternoon – I didn't want to get into bed! But then they explained to me that they were going to shoot it as if I were dreaming of playing for Ajax. That made a little more sense to me and so I flopped down on the bed and acted as best I could.

After the interview finished and the camera crew said their goodbyes I didn't think much of what had just happened. They were going back to Holland and I was staying in England. I'd never see them again. Straight away, my mind was back on football.

And on football it remained, save for the ever-increasing media requests that came my dad's way. I continued to impress for Charlden and the Harlow representative squad, starring alongside my team-mate at both clubs, future England international David Bentley. Together, we showed plenty of promise. We'd come off the pitch after games and compare how many men in big jackets with club badges we saw watching us. Scouts flocked to watch us both and we received approaches from many of the big jacketed men. "I need a word with your Dad!" they'd demand. We knew the drill, both of us pointing in the vague direction where they were standing, happy in the knowledge that we must be doing something right. Later in the car, Dad would list off who he had spoken to. "Well today we had Norwich and Ipswich and Aston Villa after you. What do you reckon? You fancy it up the Villa?"

Norwich, Ipswich and Aston Villa? None of them interested me too much. Not after my Dutch interview was released, anyway. That's the beauty of appearing on TV. You never know who's watching. Because sometimes those watching have the ability to change your life forever.

6: The Ajax Academy

AFC Ajax: the architects of total football, the home of one of the best youth development programmes in the world and, that very season, the team that would go on to win the UEFA Champions League with stars such as Marc Overmars, Edgar Davids and the De Boer brothers.

And just one club, it turned out, that took an interest in Dutch television and its quirky stories from England.

Just like any other day I walked into Dad's house and dumped my school stuff. The Dutch TV segment had aired a few weeks previously but none of us had thought much of it. There had been no viewing parties in the living room, no classroom excitement, no recognition down the park. But that was all about to change.

"There have been phone calls about you, Sonny," Dad announced from the kitchen. "We've had them from Ajax and Feyenoord. Which one do you want to go to?"

I stopped in my tracks. Ajax and Feyenoord but most importantly Ajax. Not Norwich or Ipswich or Tottenham. Ajax! Was this really happening? The team that Johan

Cruyff played for was now interested in me? The best team in the world at that moment in time?

"Ajax," I blurted out, scared the offer would be withdrawn if I waited one more second.

News travels fast. Carlton Sport, Channel 4 and Blue Peter all got in touch to ask if they could film me in action. Transworld Sport shared plans for a 30-minute documentary. Blue Peter asked to accompany me to Holland. And, of course, the *Enfield Advertiser* was full of the news.

SOCCER ACE SONNY IS ALL SET TO GO DUTCH WITH HIS IDOLS

Junior soccer ace Sonny Pike is still making a name for himself, but now, thanks to the Independent, he's finding fame in Amsterdam.

Since we started chronicling the achievements of the gifted youngster, the 11-year-old, of Willow Road, Enfield, has shown off his talents on numerous TV programmes.

Now football giants Ajax, from Amsterdam, are interested and so are The Netherlands Broadcasting Programme Foundation – the equivalent of our own BBC.

The Dutch embassy got hold of one of our own articles and they contacted the NBPF.

On Saturday an NBPF camera crew flew over to Britain to film Sonny playing for his local team, Charlden Youth, against Waltham Abbey.

Though nervous, Sonny still scored one of the goals in his team's 2-0 victory. The crew then filmed him at home, to show how he eats, sleeps and breathes football.

Sonny's dad, Mickey, said: "I couldn't believe it when the Dutch TV people phoned me up.

"I know a lot of people read the Independent but I didn't know they got it in Holland!

"Sonny is going over to Holland next year to take part in a soccer skills course and I mentioned to them that he was a big Ajax fan.

"Before you knew it we were given a free Ajax kit and I was talking to the Ajax manager on the telephone!

"He said that when Sonny comes over he will be able to train with the Ajax team.

"The telly lot got quite arty. They filmed the match first. Then they showed Sonny in bed dreaming about playing for Ajax. And then they filmed him waking up to find an Ajax football kit."

There will be more TV exposure for Sonny in December when BBC's Blue Peter films him playing football with Nottingham Forest striker Brian Roy, who used to do what Sonny wants to do – play for Ajax.

I'd never known such a buzz. It was like a whirlwind. In those weeks I walked around in a daze, still unbelieving that Ajax would offer me an opportunity. I worked harder than ever in my training sessions. Dad was great with me, taking me to the playing fields and throwing me volleys off both feet for hours. He'd always instilled a real work ethic in me and made sure I was grafting. We worked so hard that in the evenings I'd collapse onto my bed and stare around at the Ajax posters covering my bedroom walls. Everywhere I looked I could see red and white. Magazines, newspapers, books – anything that showed Ajax was ripped out and stuck up on the walls, adding to an already impressive collection.

After what felt like an eternity, the day finally arrived. My bags had been packed for days and when I returned home from school to begin the journey to Holland there were five cameramen waiting for me in my house along with a few others. "Here, Sonny," they said, "can you put that school bag back over your shoulder and walk out the front door of the house?"

"But I'm not going out of the house," I replied nonplussed.

"It'll look great on camera."

I still hadn't got the hang of acting.

The whirlwind was picking up speed. It could easily have all proved too much even then, but with Dad by my side I felt safe. He put me into situations and made me feel that I could do anything. Everything felt so safe that everything even seemed normal after a couple of takes.

Blue Peter came on the flight to Amsterdam with me and Dad. They were paying for our flights and accommodation and would then give my week-long trial an extended segment on the show.

Together we were met at Schiphol Airport in Amsterdam by Ton Pronk, Ajax's chief scout and former first-team defender with 258 appearances to his name. The first thing that hit me was his height. He was massive, certainly over six foot tall. 'Whoa, this guy is even bigger than my dad!' I thought.

Ton shook our hands and put us at ease straight away. He was a real gent. We jumped into a car with him and he showed us to our accommodation in the centre of Amsterdam. It was right in the thick of it, one of those old townhouses that rises high into the sky. Our flat was the storey right at the bottom, where the windows looked out onto the feet of the pedestrians walking along the pavement outside. Everything was so busy. The feet never stopped. Ton gave us a quick tour of the flat and then left us to it. With little sunlight making its way through the windows, me and Dad settled down into the dark flat that was our home for the next week. Straight away we set to work on making it our own, decorating it with an Ajax scarf taped to the wall and a pendant underneath. After a few more personal touches, it felt like the flat was truly ours, that we were on tour, me and Dad, here to take over Holland together. Once settled in, Dad told me about all of the media work we had to do. There was a shoot going on here, a bit of acting there. On the last day of my trial, he said, we were due to start shooting at five in the morning so the camera crews could film me training on the cobbled streets as the sun came up.

"That's a bit much," I replied. "Especially as we have a match on that last day. We could right do without that." Dad was firm with his response.

"It has to be done."

The next day I was so, so excited. I was up with the birds,

desperate for the rest of the world to wake up so my first full day in Holland could begin. When they did, Ton came to pick us up and take us to Ajax. He showed us around the stadium and the rest of the training complex. It was all in one big area south of Amsterdam, the first-team training pitch on one side of the stadium and the academy pitches on the other.

"You know, you can go and watch the first team train if you want," Ton offered. "Their session is about to start."

I didn't need asking twice. I sprinted back to the first-team training pitch and hugged this big chain link fence that separated the pitch from the outer world, my tongue hanging out as all of the players from my bedroom wall walked out before my very eyes. There were the De Boer brothers, Jari Litmanen, Nwankwo Kanu, Edgar Davids, Patrick Kluivert, Clarence Seedorf, Marc Overmars, Edwin van der Sar and the captain, Danny Blind. No wonder they were the best team in the world at that time. My eyes were popping out of my head at some of the stuff I saw. At one point in the warm-up Jari Litmanen did this skill that blew my mind, putting the ball through his legs and then dragging it back round. I'd never seen anything like it before and spent all evening trying to replicate it. By the end of that week I'd come close to nailing it.

After training finished we were taken back into the stadium and told to wait on one of the top rows of seats. The camera crew were all in place, film rolling. Suddenly, Louis van Gaal turned up and said hello, then offered us all some biscuits. I couldn't believe it! Dad, however, didn't have a clue who he was. As far as he was concerned, the Ajax manager, one of the most famous in world football, might as well have been the groundsman.

I rang Mum that afternoon to tell her all about my first morning and how brilliant it was. I told her about training, meeting everyone and the flat, and Dad not even knowing who Louis van Gaal was! Then I said about all of the filming I was going to have to do but she gave just the same response as Dad. "Do what you got to do, son. Don't worry about anything else. I'll have a word with your father."

Later that evening we returned to the Ajax complex for my first training session with the academy. I walked into that changing room and put on the same navy tracksuit with red strips down the shoulders that the first team wore. The players around me looked but didn't stare. Instead, I was the one staring at them, trying to work them out. They were different to English footballers. Much more like me in stature rather than the big units that suited the kick, bollock and bite style back home. I said my hellos to them and then sat down on the changing room bench and stared at the Ajax badge on my chest. That's when it sunk in. The enormity of the situation. I was actually about to go and train with Ajax, just as Johan Cruyff had all those years ago.

The Ajax academy coach entered the room and gave his instructions in Dutch, then translated them into English for my benefit. He was in his 30s and had straight, blond hair styled into curtains, as was the fashion at the time. After translating, he encouraged one of the other players, a kid called Rohan, to look after me. Rohan was an English speaker and with that knowledge I made sure to stay close to him when we got out onto the pitch.

I never usually got nervous when I played football but this was an exception. I was so desperate to impress. It didn't even matter that there were film crews training their cameras on me. All I cared about was doing myself justice while wearing the famous Ajax badge.

We warmed up with plenty of small, technical movements. The coach gave us each a ball and we were off. He explained first to the others in Dutch, then he'd switch instantly. "And Sonny, we're going to do this." I'm glad he did explain, because if I hadn't heard him tell me in English what we were going to do I'd have thought my new team-mates were mad. They dribbled their balls around while clapping their hands above their heads. A little baffled, I gave it a go and quickly realised why the coach was making us dribble like that. Removing the hands put more emphasis on the connection between foot and ball. Clapping while dribbling improved co-ordination and forced you to keep your head up. From there, the coach progressed the session and got us to do lots of little skills. He'd call out the name of a skill and every kid would execute it flawlessly on his command. Inside hooks, stop turns, Cruyff turns, all on either foot, it was just like I was back in Aldersbrook Park. I fitted in immediately.

After the technical drills came the game to end the training session. Only, I couldn't see any goals. Instead, the coach brought out these tiny little things, about one foot high and one foot wide, and plonked them at either end. What was going on? The ball would hardly be able to fit in the net. While I was still searching for the actual goals, the game started. This was normal at Ajax. They were light years ahead of England, where kids played in full-size goals, chasing after the ball on full-size pitches. Those tiny goals, I found, gave even more emphasis on players' skill. You couldn't just hit and hope. You had to be certain you could score, and for that you had to play much more of a pass-and-move game in the hope of opening up your opponent's defence. As I demanded the ball from my new team-mates I lost myself in the game. Nothing outside the pitch mattered. It was just me and the ball and a load of kids in navy tracksuits with red stripes who were just like me. Kids who were technical players. Kids who were slender. Kids who wanted to get on the ball and spray it around with either foot. It didn't matter that I was English and they were Dutch. All that mattered was the game.

The more I played, the more I realised I could fit in.

The Dutch style suited me much better. I'd said it over and over again on all of those interviews but now I was here those words actually rung true. The emphasis on the technical rather than the physical suited me right down to the ground. Maybe I could make something of myself over in Holland at the best academy in the world. Maybe this was for me.

I was so caught up in the play that when the coach blew his whistle to end the session and Tim Vincent came to congratulate me and award me my official Blue Peter badge, I'd forgotten all about the people watching on. The film crew might as well have been pointing their cameras the other way for all I cared. I'd loved the training session that much and I couldn't wait to do it all over again.

Two more training sessions followed before the match that was due to conclude my week-long trial. They were much the same formula, both focused on the technical details that Johan Cruyff preached. As a result, the technical standard of the players was high. All of the play was nice and tight and everyone looked good, but I felt that nobody stood out too much ahead of me. I was comfortable and knew that parts of my play had impressed.

In between training sessions the film crew made sure they got their money's worth from me. Further trips to the stadium for transition shots and filler content were added to interviews and clips of me training by myself in obscure places. Moments to myself were few and far between. Any downtime was spent not relaxing but worrying about all of the next commitments I had. There was never a chance to switch off. There was always a training session to film or a match to play in or a tourist site to explore. Not even when the camera crews left their cameras behind and we all went into the centre of Amsterdam for an evening meal together could we properly relax.

"Dad, what are them women doing in the windows?" I asked. That wasn't the only tough question my dad had to field that evening as we walked past the Red Light District on the way to the Chinese restaurant we had booked into on one of the canals. He was similarly stumped on the way back when we stopped off at a corner shop to buy a drink.

Above the counter there were silver packets with women's knickers in them. "What are they doing?" I asked, entirely innocently.

On my final day, the moment I'd been dreading arrived. At 5am our alarm went off, giving us just enough time to get ready for sun rise. As the sun rose on what was the biggest day of my life, the day I'd play a proper game for Ajax, I found myself dribbling a ball down the cobbled streets of Amsterdam for the cameras instead of preparing for my match. From left foot to right foot, Cruyff turn to keepie-ups, every base was covered on those cobbled streets. Yet still we needed to film more. They took us to the Amsterdam Flower Market on one of the many canals in the city centre, then to some of the other sites. Skills were followed by interviews, which were followed by footage of me and Dad sitting down and chatting. It wasn't until midday that the call came through to cut filming.

Two hours later I found myself lined up on a pitch wearing the red and white kit of Ajax, the coach giving us all a team talk for the match ahead. The team-mates I'd trained with for the previous week, as well as a couple of trialists, surrounded me. I doubted that many of them had prepared for the game with a seven-hour workday.

We drew the match 1-1 and I scored our goal with a strike from outside the box. It made for great content for the film crew who had the benefit of cutting and editing to create their documentary. The reality, though, was that I hadn't played anywhere near as well as I knew I could. Even in the warm-up I had felt knackered, and in the match my energy levels were far below the usual. Not even a goal from outside the box could paper over the cracks.

Still, I left the pitch with a smile on my face. The whole Ajax experience had undoubtedly been the best week of my life. My confidence had reached new limits after holding my own in the best academy in the world. It gave me the desire to return to England and push on.

Signing for Ajax had never been part of the plan. I was just a kid and couldn't have left my mum on her own back in England. But even so, part of me wanted Ajax to make an offer. Plenty of nice things had been said about me by the coaching staff. Ton Pronk had even told my dad that my reading of the game was at an advanced level. "If he doesn't make it as a player, he's got all of the attributes to coach," he had said as Dad shook him by the hand.

We were both full of smiles on the plane back. Our little team on our away tour had done its best to conquer Holland and put up a good fight.

"This has been brilliant," I said to Dad. "I loved it. But I can't wait to get back to normal football each week now. Just football and nothing else."

"Yeah, yeah, yeah," came the response. "We're going to keep it all football now."

A week later a letter arrived at my mum's house in Willow Road, Enfield. Dad had been expecting it and once again, the film crew were back. That hadn't fitted in with my plan, but I still appreciated they had to finish the documentary. I could allow them that.

We all gathered outside in the garden, Dad, Mum, me and

my two sisters. It was like we were our own proper, normal family again. It made me so happy to see them all together, smiling and getting along. 'If I keep succeeding then maybe I can get my family back together permanently,' I thought. The reunion had, as always, been brought about for the benefit of the cameras, but the more reunions there were the greater the chances of togetherness. I wanted it to happen just as much as I wanted to be a footballer.

Dad opened the letter and inspected it quickly. It was all very official, the Ajax logo stamped onto the letterhead. He then read it out for the benefit of all of us. Sonny is a good player, the letter read, but in this Ajax team he isn't better than what we already have. We can see his potential and so we would like to keep monitoring him. To help us do this, we would like him to come to Ajax a couple of times a year.

The cameras were trained on me the whole time, waiting for my reaction. They focused in on the Ajax logo. As Dad read out Ton Pronk's sign-off from the letter I couldn't help but smile once again. Dad came and put his arm round me and told me how proud he was. Mum was in the background echoing Dad's words. It was a really nice family moment of shared success.

But then the cameras all went and the illusion was over. My sisters left, Mum went inside the house and Dad returned to his home. I was alone again, the family no longer together. The contents of the letter were whirring around inside my head.

'If I can impress at Ajax, I can impress anywhere,' I thought over and over again.

In that moment, I'd never been more sure that I was going to make it as a professional footballer. Now all I had to do was shoot for the stars.

7: Stardom

"Don't send the boy away, he will make us proud some day," the man across from me sang. Energised and letting the rhythm course through his veins, his pink face was getting pinker with every syllable. It was me that he was singing about. Me. And here I was in the studio with him, my dad on the other side of the plexiglass, nodding along to the beat and urging me to go along with it.

I breathed in, calmed my nerves and waited for the signal. The chorus ended and then it arrived. I exploded, methodically shouting the lines that had been created for me without thinking of much else.

All I need is a school for skill,

I don't want to work in some moneyman's drill.

It wasn't exactly going to be troubling Oasis for airtime on Top of the Pops. Nor was it quite in the same style as the House of Pain album I'd bought from HMV on my final day in Amsterdam and hadn't stopped playing since. But Dad seemed pleased. Along with my new friend the singer – a man by the name of Basil Simonenko – and my new agent, Tony Nunn, he was convinced that it would be a Top 40 hit. They'd make a killing. Of course it was going to be a success. Tony was behind it, the showbiz agent who handled Michael Jackson's UK interests at the time. And after all, Dad added, I'd need something to fall back on if the football didn't work out.

Rapping didn't seem the obvious Plan B and I pulled him up on it, but Dad eventually managed to convince me to go ahead with it by showing me the Liverpool players singing their 'Anfield Rap', which they released before their 1988 FA Cup final against Wimbledon.

Once we were done I shrugged, content that I'd made them happy but eager to get back to what truly made me happy: football.

Only, football was now proving harder to come by. What media interest I'd had before I went to Ajax had exploded. Television, radio, newspapers, sponsors, events; it seemed to be a new thing every day, all eating into the time I could have been dedicating to the beautiful game. I even had not just one agent in Tony, but two agents, the second a northern man by the name of Mark Steele who was coordinating with Tony and my dad's approval. I'd gone up to Mark's house to do this photo shoot that he had arranged to create a portfolio of me, which he then planned to send to prospective brands and media outlets. There were loads of different outfits for me to pose in and I ended up being properly impressed. Mark lived in a great big house with an enormous back garden that led on to a river. The most impressive part, however, was the interior. Mark took me and my dad inside and gave us the tour, showing us these fancy light switches he'd installed that changed the whole colour of the room. Press one button and the room transformed to a deep shade of red, another and it became a royal blue. My mouth wide open, I pulled on Dad's sleeve. "Look at this geezer's house, Dad," I whispered, awestruck. I felt like I was in Willy Wonka's chocolate factory, that any second an Oompa-Loompa would burst out of a wardrobe juggling a football with Augustus Gloop in tow.

To be honest, it wouldn't have been too much of a surprise because my post-Ajax reality proved to be beyond my wildest dreams. Prior to my trial I was seen as a promising kid with potential, but that's all. There are thousands of promising kids with potential. Every local area has a load of them at each age group. But then Ajax came along and all of a sudden I was the real deal. I was better than Best – that was for sure – and under my dad's guidance I was destined for greatness. The English Maradona. Enfield's own Gazza. Everyone I came across agreed that future stardom was an inevitability.

And here I was, a 12-year-old kid from suburbia trying to stay on track as life rushed by. 'British Soccer's Brightest Shooting Star', 'An Exceptional Talent', 'Remember The Name', 'Simply The Best…That's Sonny'. There were even reports that the England manager, Terry Venables, had said that I was the next Ryan Giggs, which was the exact headline splashed across the front of *The Big Issue*, along with a massive photo of me in my Ajax kit. '*His play has Cantona's depth, and the speed of Andrei Kanchelskis,*' the article gushed. *The Daily Telegraph* summed up the nation's mood as it asked 'Is this 12-year-old boy wonder our football hope?' on its front page. No matter how many interviews I did, there were always more to come. The media couldn't get enough. It even went beyond just reporting on my footballing ability. 'Soccer's boy wonder has the girls interested too!' crowed the *Enfield Independent* as it reported that I had 'more in common with his hero George Best – he is also proving to be just as successful with the ladies'.

The coverage marked a more general awakening amongst the nation's sports media. The days when footballers were just footballers were on their way out. In the wake of Sky's mammoth television deal, the status of footballers was slowly beginning to shift. Formerly confined to the back pages, an interest was starting to develop in their previously private lives. A new type of fan was emerging, one which sat in the stands wearing the same shirt as the players out on the pitch having paid a rapidly increasing entry fee for the privilege. Football was becoming fashionable; its players were no longer purely sportsmen – they were entertainers. And it was mad. I was a 12-year-old kid and people actually cared whether or not I was a hit with the girls at school.

Having finished primary school at Forty Hill, that summer I had moved to the secondary school round the corner from home: Chace Community. Whether or not I was a hit with the girls was out of the question, because any chance I got I played football on the playground rather than speak to the opposite sex, but there were certainly more girls about than at my previous school. Chace couldn't have been more the opposite of Forty Hill primary school. Forty Hill was a tiny school where everyone knew everyone. Chace Community was massive, a proper old-school comprehensive with a great big drafty assembly hall and a main building from the 1950s that was three floors tall in parts. There were more than 200 kids in every school year, the years so big that they had to be split in half depending on whether you chose to study French or German. There was only one pupil from Forty Hill, a girl called Gemma who got put into the same form group as me. Most of the intake came from the biggest local primary school, Lavender. They were used to big, but even Chace Community felt big to them. To me and Gemma, it was ginormous. For the first week, we clutched on to the map of the school that came in our planners. It felt crazy that people knew where to go, that anybody could know all of the parts of a school as big as this.

Aware that the transition from small to big may prove challenging, Dad sat me down on the eve of my first day and gave me some clear advice. "Always be yourself. Never try and impress anyone. Never be a sheep. Stand up for yourself. Don't let anyone talk down to you. Never let anyone bully you. When you go to Chace you might have some trouble. Kids might want to fight you. Now, you never want to be known as the toughest kid in the school but you need to let people know they can't take liberties with ya. So if you hear that a kid wants to fight you, I don't care what you're doing, if you're in the middle of a lesson or whatever, you get up and go and find that kid. Walk up to him and asks if he wants trouble with you. If he says 'no' then turn around and walk away. If he says 'yes' then fucking hit him as hard as you can. If he says 'erm, I don't know' what should you do?"

"I don't know."

"Fucking hit him as hard as you can. Fucking hit him as hard as you can. Fucking hit him as hard as you can."

It couldn't have been any further from Mum's advice. She was massively into the concept of karma, treating others as you'd like to be treated. Gentle. A totally relaxed vibe. Getting the balance between Dad's go-go-go nature and Mum's calmness was often my hardest challenge.

But thanks to football, the transition was easy. A lot of my mates from down the park went to Chace. A lot of kids I'd played with at Enfield and Charlden were there. More importantly, I was the brother of Dominique Pike. After her Grange Hill appearance, my sister had gone on to achieve legendary status at the school, increased only further when she was expelled from the school in the months following her TV debut. Within weeks of that appearance she was living like an adult, going out drinking with people notably older than her, hanging around with the wrong crowd, missing school. Having Year 11s recognise you and shout your name in the playground can do wonders for a new starter at a school – especially in warding off people who wanted to fight you. Most important, however, was the whole media hype that followed Ajax. At Forty Hill, my classmates acknowledged my football skills and Mr Craig and Mrs Moore always made a point of asking me how I was getting on with my football. But at Chace the attention was a whole new level. The pupils went nuts. I soon got used to them throwing open windows and screaming my name, rushing up to me and asking me to sign their planners. I felt like Michael Jackson! Even the older kids, the ones from down the park such as Andrew and Phil, were coming up and congratulating me. "You're the man," they would say when they saw me in the school corridors or in the playground. "What you're doing is unbelievable." Yet the most unbelievable thing for me was that these older kids who were practically men, the ones that I'd spent so long looking up to in the park were now looking up to me, saying it was amazing what I'd done.

With such support around the school, it didn't take long to make new friends. Soon enough I felt comfortable at my new school, fitting in like everyone else by playing football and wearing the look of the day: a record bag as a school bag and either an Eclipse or Spliffy jacket over my school uniform. Mum used to hate the jacket that I chose, a Spliffy one with a guy smoking on it. "Take that bloody thing off!" she'd yell. The kids in the playground loved it, though. After a few kickabouts on the playground in my new jacket I had my new group: Ben, Gary, Arran and Roy. Ben was a friend from nursery, tall and slim with brown hair and freckles. A Spurs fan who lived just up the road from me and was into his golf, Ben possessed a dry sense of humour. Arran was also into his golf as well as football. Roy went over to Enfield FC each week with his dad and would even start some of the fans' chants off himself, which really impressed all of us. We were in loads of lessons together and always had a laugh when we could. Gary, in particular, even became my protector, doing his best to shake off the two girls that followed me home from school every day. "Leave him alone, he ain't interested!" he'd shout back at the blonde and brunette a few paces behind us who delighted in whispering my name. My cheeks would flare up – I'd be too embarrassed to speak to them – but Gary had no issues. He didn't mind going against the grain in class either. Science was a particular frustration of ours. We used to hate it. During one lesson the teacher, Mr Conway, went out of the classroom briefly. In that moment, the two of us ran up to the front and wound the clock forward by 50 minutes. By the time he came back in, we were back in our seats. We wasted no time in telling him we'd run out of time for the lesson. Mr Conway looked over at the clock and saw that yes, he had in fact run out of time. The class was dismissed, with me and Gary laughing all the way down the corridor and out of school.

Usually, I didn't have to get so creative to miss lessons. In Year Seven my attendance was well under 50 per cent. If ever there was a clash between football and school, Dad chose football. If ever there was clash between media work and school there was absolutely no question. In the two-and-a-half months after my Ajax experience, I was the subject of 64 media events. Sometimes the commitments would take up the whole day, other times there would be at least three or four interviews crammed into a single day.

Occasionally it would all get too much for me. There was one particular shoot with *Hello!* magazine where I had an overwhelming desire to sleep as I was made to pose in different positions whilst the camera pointed at me. I hadn't napped that day – a new routine that was becoming ever more essential with my commitments – and was suffering the consequences. Napping became normal. Essential. Yet on that particular day I was just a tired kid and to me *Hello!* had no real meaning.

It wasn't like it was *Fully Booked*, a show which I really loved going on. I watched it every week and so to suddenly appear on it was crazy. They flew me up to Scotland on a private plane and put me on at the same time as the Australian singer Peter Andre, whose *Mysterious Girl* single had just been released. The show was hosted by Kate Kendall, the actress who played Lauren Carpenter in *Neighbours*, a soap I liked watching. After the show, Peter Andre handed me one of his CDs and signed it for me. *Take it to the top, champ*, he'd written before squiggling his name below.

I did so many appearances that I was often told I was a natural. To be honest, it would have been impossible not to have been. For the first few shows I was nervous but once you've done a couple you become fairly comfortable. Though I'd rather have been out on the football pitch the appearances were often still enjoyable. There was one where Subbuteo invited me down to Wembley Arena to do the draw for the Subbuteo European Championships with Lee Dixon. I played Subbuteo at home so that was right up my street. They got the pair of us up to the front and gave us a big sack which contained a load of different balls. It was our job to swish the balls around, then select one and therefore select the ties. There must have been at least 50 ties to select and I loved every second. It felt like I was doing the FA Cup draw! There was a music video with Mark Morrison, of *Return of the Mack* fame, where we spent the day filming in a mansion, which led to an offer from Simply Red to appear in their *Fairground* music video. Then there was David Baddiel and Frank Skinner's *Fantasy Football League* on the BBC, a television programme that couldn't have been more 1990s if it tried. Mum came along to that one with me and Dad, which was strange because she rarely came along to anything I did with the media unless it was at our house. Try as they might, Baddiel and Skinner couldn't convince her to appear on the show with me, so instead they dressed up this random woman to come on whilst they were interviewing me and march me off stage for "going too close to that Statto bloke". It was funny but the whole time I was thinking, 'Who's this strange woman?'

With every spare second I was able to get I'd have a football at my feet. I'd often race back from a media commitment and hunt down Terry, who Dad had asked to be my new one-on-one coach. Always happy to help out talented young footballers, Terry agreed and didn't even charge. At first, our sessions were regular: three or four evenings a week, all lasting an hour over on the playing fields at Chace. Terry's philosophy remained unchanged from his mass training sessions by Southbury Road. "A ball, a ball, a ball," he'd recite as I went about the technical drills he set me. "Technique, technique, technique." Left foot, right foot, inside, outside, against the wall, round the cones. Proper warm-ups, followed by plenty of touches using all parts of each foot. "Know your stuff, never bluff," Terry would remind me as he taught the correct technique to use. "If you can't pass a ball, you can't play football" when playing one-twos with the wall. "A steady head is the golden thread that runs through football" while shooting.

When Terry's words weren't enough, he'd sometimes modify my training to emphasise a point. To improve my weak foot he made me take off my right boot so I would have to use my left foot all the time. "It's all about the five Ps," he'd say, "Proper Preparation Prevents Poor Performance." That was why we always had to warm up so thoroughly. That was why he prepared me properly by teaching me all of the essentials. Not just improving my passing, control, dribbling and shooting, but teaching me how to find space off the ball, to make an angle, have the body shape to receive the ball, to never stand still, to create, to improvise, to always move, always look for the ball, to change direction. "It's the principles of play," he'd say. 'Penetration, mobility, width, improvisation, delay, balance, control."

Terry was years ahead of his time. I absolutely loved his sessions. We worked hard, getting thousands of touches of the ball at a time, but Terry never ran me ragged. He was always more worried about technique. "You kids bloody run around enough in school, you don't need to do that in training," he'd say in his wise old way. "Fitness comes and goes but you never lose technique."

When we finished each session, Terry would walk me

back home and teach me all about self-improvement off the pitch. "What you been eating then?" he'd ask. If I ever told him I'd had a McDonald's he'd go nuts. "McDonalds?!" he'd scream. "Bloody hamburgers! Chips? They're just potatoes with their heads kicked in!" Terry strongly believed that footballers had to live well away from the pitch, getting plenty of rest and eating plenty of greens. On our walks he'd pick all sorts of wild berries off the trees and flowers from the ground. "You can eat this, you know," he'd say before popping one in his mouth. He would tell me the names of the plants and what they would do. He even told me that in the army he ate stinging nettles. That's how I knew he was a little mad. "You'll never believe this old man," I raced home and told Mum. "He says you can eat stinging nettles!" Mum just smiled.

I soon became close with Terry. Our training sessions became the highlight of my weeks. He'd often bring along Paul Furlong, who was playing for Chelsea at that point, for me to train alongside. A favourite game of ours was football tennis.

At the same time I'd spend days when I should have been in school at the snooker rooms in Enfield and ended up playing alongside another of Paul's team-mates at Chelsea, Michael Duberry. Me and Terry would spend plenty of time together away from the pitch. One weekend, as a late birthday treat, he took me down to London to buy a new pair of boots. We went into a sports shop in Carnaby Street and Terry walked straight up to the shop assistant and gave him a nudge.

"You know who that is?" he said, pointing at me. "That's Sonny Pike. He's sponsored by you lot."

"Oh yeah?" the assistant replied, much to Terry's delight. He was hoping to get a decent discount.

"He's interested in getting a pair of boots. How about those ones up there?" Terry pointed onto the shelf at a Nike pair costing £50.

"Okay, great," the assistant said. "That'll be £50 please."

As my weeks became increasingly taken up with media work, however, training with Terry took a hit.

"Come on, Terry," I'd say after racing home from a shoot. "Let's train."

"Not today, son, not today," he'd sometimes reply. I was always gutted when he said that. It really baffled me. Why wouldn't he work with me? After all, I'd had my nap in the car. But nothing I said could change his mind. Instead of training, he'd just take my dog Winston out for a walk. Back then I didn't understand that Terry was teaching me about the importance of rest. I didn't realise that a nap in the car between a shoot and training wasn't the same as rest. I couldn't work out that Terry had my best interests at heart. As a keen and committed kid with seemingly boundless energy – on the football field at least – I always felt like I could train every hour of the day.

The training I was managing to do with Terry was helping me to progress even further on the pitch. I was well on course to break my record of 120 goals in a season. My stock swelled by the Ajax experience, I'd been contacted by pretty much every club going. Manchester United,

Ipswich, Norwich, Tottenham, Crystal Palace, QPR, the list was endless. As a precaution, my legs were insured for £1 million. Soon, however, I found the precaution was a necessity. The sidelines could get fiery at the best of times in the win-at-all-costs grassroots level. Opposition managers and parents would always encourage their players and kids to go in to tackles hard, to "take him out". When they saw me lining up against them, however, the aggression went up to a whole new level – even in school football. Some of what they said was just plain abuse. "Fucking kick him, he's shit!" "Break his legs – he'll get a million quid!" "Take him the fuck out!"

It almost became a competition to see who could break my legs first. Tackles came in from all angles and the guardians of the game – the grown men and women, the parents and teachers and coaches who were supposed to be promoting fair play and protecting those on the pitch – tended to be the ones shouting. "Corr, that was uncomfortable today," my team-mates would comment. I could have shrunk inside myself in such a situation, but to me the screams from the sidelines just added fuel to the fire. I became even more desperate to teach them a lesson. The wild slide tackles did wonders for my awareness and reading of the game. I developed a sixth sense for when I was in danger, learning to jump over the challenges and maintain control of the ball. The best way to shut them up, however, was to score a goal. In one particular game, Terry, watching on from the sidelines, became incensed at the behaviour of the opposition's manager. "Take him out!" the manager screamed over and over again as I slalomed past his defenders. Eventually, Terry had enough and stormed around the pitch to give the manager a piece of his mind, only to bump into me as I readied myself to take a corner.

"Don't worry about him, Terry. Watch this." With that I bent the corner straight into the top of the net. "That'll shut 'em up," I assured him. Terry's face wasn't half a picture after that.

More often than not, I managed to shut them up by scoring. But even if I did have a stinker or failed to score or hid inside myself, I was always safe in the knowledge that Dad had no qualms about fighting the adults who were giving the most abuse. I knew that because he told me before every match. "Shut them up, Sonny. And if you don't shut them up on the pitch, I'll shut them up for you."

That £1 million blessing was both an insurance and a curse. While it egged on my most aggressive opponents, it did at least give something to fall back on should the worst happen. I never did find out which agent the bright idea was down to because I seemed to have a different agent every month. The changes in agent led to all kinds of offers, which led to all kinds of strange experiences. Tony Nunn became Mark Steele who became Mark Curtis. He got me a game for Sunderland, which didn't seem the ideal team to play for when pretty much every team in the Premier League was offering me a place. Still, Dad wanted to meet Mark Curtis and so play for Sunderland I did. Together we drove up the A1, all the way to Sunderland's stadium. "Off you go then," Dad said, shepherding me onto a team bus full of young Mackems while he jumped into a fancy-looking Jaguar. I'd been put into lots of random situations by then and was used to being around people I didn't know. I was never one for starting random conversations and bouncing around a room, but I was quietly confident. If ever someone I didn't know started a conversation with me I'd be happy to speak with them. The Sunderland players were all a bit nonplussed as to why Sonny Pike was on their minibus, but they welcomed me into the team for the two-hour journey back down south to play against Sheffield Wednesday. When we arrived in Sheffield it was pissing it down with rain. I got stuck in the middle of the park, a position I'd never played in before, but gave a good account of myself in a 1-1 draw. Ajax academy it certainly wasn't. Gone were the slender, technical players, replaced by English intensity and brute force. On the ball I stood out, off it I wasn't quite as impressive. Dad and his new friend Mark Curtis watched the game from the Jaguar before driving all the way back to Sunderland so me and Dad could then drive back south again, this time home to Enfield.

Sunderland was never a realistic option for me. Just as quickly as he'd arrived, Mark Curtis disappeared and another agent turned up, along with a load more offers from near and far. Dad loved speaking to all of the different agents, finding out how they could help us, what connections they could give him, how they could achieve his dream of making Sonny Pike a star.

Playing for Charlden was one of the few constants in the period of media and agent madness. I couldn't wait to just get on the grass and play, putting into practice all that I'd learned with Terry that week. If it was down to me, all that I'd done was play. The media appearances could be fun, the agents could be interesting, but they weren't football.

Gradually, I got involved with more local teams – when time would allow. Dad heard from someone that Leyton Orient had a reputation for developing youngsters and so he took me along to train with their youth team. Despite all that was happening, Dad thought it important I remained humble. He believed it important we didn't rush. After all, I could sign with one of the big boys when I was older. And after all, it'd be much harder to maintain media interest if I'd already selected the big club I was going to play for. Better to keep it small and maintain the interest.

I took straight to life at Orient. There were a few nerves there in my first game as I knew it was a bit of step up. Dad made a point that it wasn't Sunday League anymore, but in the end there was no need to worry. At their training facility just off the A13 I scored twice as we won my first match 4-2. Within a few weeks I was the team's top scorer.

In addition to Charlden, Orient and the Harlow League representative side, I had also been called up to play for the East Anglian representative team. That was seen as a special privilege. There was an awards ceremony to announce the selection with Ray Parlour there as the guest of honour. It was Ray's job to give a speech and then welcome all of the new players into the East Anglia squad. Two of us received the call-up from the Harlow League representative team, myself and David.

There were grand rules around the East Anglia team. We were given special ties with the East Anglian crest on and had to turn up to official commitments in suits. The Paul Smith connection really helped me out there. Every month there would be a commitment. Usually they were representative games, but occasionally they'd just be training camps up in Norwich where we could learn from our coach, Martin Lacey. He was a right nice fella, tall with dark hair, who absolutely lived and breathed football. The rumour was that he had good connections with Arsenal and Watford, and a couple of our players were involved in the youth set-ups at those clubs, as well as at West Ham, Norwich and Ipswich. After the first few meet-ups, myself and David emerged as the stronger players alongside a promising winger called Ashley Young.

Before every meet-up, Dad would emphasise the importance of what was about to happen. "They pick the England schoolboys' team from this, you know. Be the best here and you can get a chance with England."

And eventually, in a way, that chance came. The Dana Cup, known as the Mini Youth World Cup, pitted teams from all over the globe against each other. East Anglia, it turned out, would be England's representative. The players were all buzzing. So were the parents. The tournament wasn't free to take part in, but everyone found a way to cover their costs. Dad started spreading the word that he'd had to sell his car to cover the cost of the tournament. I didn't ever find out if that was true or not. He'd always be bouncing around different flats and have different cars anyway. Once, he even turned up in a three-wheeler, just like Del Boy from *Only Fools and Horses*.

The squad headed out to Denmark full of hope. Preparation had stepped up a level and the team was looking strong. From David's creativity in the middle to my goals up top, we knew we stood a chance against representatives from Belgium, Denmark, Germany, Holland, Poland, Russia, Sweden and the United States.

All eyes were on our opponents. And yet, crazily, many of their eyes were on me. Even walking down the corridors of our accommodation in the northern town of Hjørring I couldn't escape recognition. A group of players from the American team swarmed me one evening, all of them screaming my name and brandishing pens and magazines. "Sonny! Sonny! Will you sign this for us?" they asked.

Bloody hell.

I looked down and saw them clutching copies of *Shoot* and *Disney* magazines, all opened to glossy pages from which my face was beaming out of. I wasn't half taken aback. Here I was, speaking with people from the other side of the world, who were playing in the same competition as me, and they wanted my autograph. What did they want that for? I really didn't know what to say – I was so surprised – but went about signing their magazines anyway, all the while thinking how strange their accents were.

Our first game was against Russia and I was given the honour of captaining the side. As part of the formalities, I had to give a British pendant to my Russian counterpart and received a Russian one in return. It all felt very proper and important, and those feelings only increased as we won game after game until a very English semi-final defeat. In the third-place play-off we were up against a Polish team in front of a sizeable crowd, but any feelings of nerves soon gave way as I scored twice to give us a 3-1 victory and finish the tournament as the Golden Boot winner with 23 goals – nine clear of the second top scorer. What an unbelievable feeling! After each goal I hunted out my mate David and the two of us would run off to do the celebration made popular by Ryan Giggs and Lee Sharpe. We'd planned it perfectly in our efficient accommodation in Hjørring, having plenty of laughs, but to do it in the Mini World Cup was something else!

As we danced around in celebration, laughing and joking, the Americans were back amongst it screaming my name. I still found it mad that I could be recognised when I went away from Enfield, let alone England, but it was a feeling I soon had to get used to. Weeks later I attended a five-a-side tournament down in Bournemouth, playing as a ringer for a team called Street Youth. Teams came from all over for a chance of glory. Straight away, it got out that Sonny Pike was on a team. People recognised me. There were nudges, whispers and gestures in my direction. Then a whole new rumour did the rounds: the scorpion kick geezer is here! After hearing that, Dad told me to go and see if the rumour was true. "Find him," he urged me. It didn't take me long. Rene Higuita was instantly recognisable, his bleached blond, long curly barnet even more unique than my own. The former Colombian keeper, famous for his flair and especially his scorpion kick, a move where he jumped up, lifted his heels above his head and batted the ball away with his feet, had recently become infamous after being locked up in a Colombian jail for nine months. He'd been accused, falsely he insisted, of being the mediator in one of Pablo Escobar's kidnappings. He later told newspapers that he sued the state and won over his incarceration, but he was notorious at the time. What he was doing in Bournemouth was anyone's guess – although it later crossed my mind that he could have just been a lookalike! I made my way over and introduced myself. When the two of us were seen together, in the same place, it went out of control. An announcement went out for the security guards to come over to us. From that moment on, they had to escort us between games for the rest of the day so we didn't have to fight through the crowds. When my team made the final, a large crowd gathered. People were spilling over the sides and fighting for any space they could find. "And here come our first finalists, Sonny Pike!" the man on the megaphone announced. Not Street Youth, but Sonny Pike. They'd renamed our team once they discovered I – a ringer – was playing on it. With the pressure on I managed to bag our winner in the last minute, sending the place into pandemonium. People were rushing onto the pitch and lifting me onto their shoulders.

Such increasing recognition wasn't being missed by those around me. If I hadn't realised the impact my media appearances were having then businesses certainly were. The increasing interest in football that had catapulted the increasing media space given to footballers presented a unique opportunity for companies. Here was a chance for them to associate their brand with an active, wholesome pursuit. Well-known footballers, fit and healthy role models as they were, could be seen with their products to help the business increase sales. And as England's young hope – according to *The Daily Telegraph*, anyway – I was in demand.

8: The Sky is the Limit

Dear Sir/Madam,

I am making enquiries reference my son 'Sonny'. Sonny is a 12-year-old talented footballer. He has been approached by several premier division football clubs and is already tipped to become a future high-class star. However! Sonny is not interested in signing for any club in England as of yet, but wishes to learn the continental style of the game, which he feels will give him a better education for the future.

Sonny has had trials with Ajax, the Dutch European champions, and has been invited back for future assessments and training.

Apart from this, Sonny is already high profile, and has appeared on many TV shows including BBC, Channel 4, Sky TV and Transatlantic Sport. Also, he has done radio programmes. Over the next year, Sonny will be visiting countries all over Europe, and in July next year will be playing in the USA.

In order to finance these trips and also to pay for special training and for the training venues he must use, I am seeking sponsorship in return for the advertising of products (Sonny is very photogenic).

I am therefore enquiring as to whether your company can see Sonny in any future advertising campaigns? It should be noted that Sonny has also appeared in the national press including Mail on Sunday and the Guardian.

I am enclosing a photograph of Sonny and would be grateful if you would contact myself, by letter or indeed by telephone on the numbers given, as soon as possible.

I remain yours sincerely,

Mickey Pike.

I'd never heard of Mizuno but Mizuno had heard of me and that was all that mattered. After a few phone calls with whichever agent was representing me – it could have been one of any – and my dad, Mizuno was the first big brand to get me on board. I say big brand because I'd been fortunate enough to have two sponsors before everything blew up.

Before Ajax, my dad had written to a number of local businesses, telling them how he had a talented son who needed extra financial support to get to the next level. Briggs, a local sports shop in Enfield, was the first to respond and provided me with tracksuits and training kit. Dad also managed to get Charlie Magri, the former world champion boxer from London's East End, to throw in a couple of hundred pounds along with some kit. Both were instrumental in supporting me on my journey to

Holland, and almost as soon as I returned Dad sharpened his pen once again in the hunt for more sponsorship. The continental angle worked, he realised. By getting me to say I wanted to play abroad, it interested the media, and interest in the media became interest from businesses, and interest from businesses meant money, and money and fame and attention meant the big time: celebrity. Stardom.

The second time round it was much easier. Especially once he got the agents involved. Dad soon enough received contact from a lady called Cathy Fryer. She was in charge of sponsorships at Mizuno and invited us to their headquarters. We went and were both blown away – eventually. Cathy greeted us and she made us really welcome. She had a friendly persona, really kind and caring, and showed us around the grounds. We started off at the blue plaque with Mizuno's logo at the front of the complex, then went into their big shiny main building where there were loads of people tapping away on computers. 'What have they brought me here for?' I wondered. What was the point of me being in an office? But then Cathy took us into a back room and I realised. She invited us both to sit, and then a steady procession of staff came into the room with different Mizuno catalogues. There were catalogues dedicated to football boots, to trainers, to training kit, to leisure wear.

"Circle whatever you like," Cathy told me.

"What, like, anything?"

She nodded and smiled. I grabbed the big magic marker that had been placed next to me and I was off. Boom, boom,

boom. Circle, circle, circle. I'll have that tracksuit, that T-shirt, those boots, yeah, that ball looks nice, I'll take three of them. I couldn't believe it. Cathy gave me absolutely no restrictions. If there were eight of an item then I'd circle four. I could get the same T-shirt in loads of different colours. In the end, I circled so much stuff I didn't know what I could do with it all.

"Leave it to us," Cathy smiled. While we were eating lunch, she sent her colleagues off with my catalogues. Later that day they returned with heaps of free product plucked from the shelves. Anything they didn't have in stock they promised to send to my mum's house. They were true to their word.

From that day Mizuno was my boot sponsor. As part of the agreement I had to actively promote Mizuno, wearing their gear and taking part in shoots for commercials. That was no problem, because the boxes carried on coming to the house. I had more Mizuno stuff than I knew what to do with. Mizuno were good as gold. They had a few other footballers on their books such as Gianfranco Zola and Dwight Yorke. Yet they always seemed to go out of their way for me. They even created a new pair of boots especially for me and Yorke. We both had the wonderkid label and so Mizuno manufactured a gold pair of boots for the two of us, which we both had exclusive access to for a year before they hit the mass market.

Hot on the heels of Mizuno came Coca-Cola. They made contact with Dad through one of the many agents and then called us in to their London office and sat me down in their meeting room. A marketing executive then proceeded to tell me how Coca-Cola was investing heavily in football. The League Cup was officially known as The Coca-Cola League Cup and there was a big campaign around the corner for Euro 96 with the catchy slogan of 'Eat Football, Sleep Football, Drink Coca-Cola'. This was all illustrated with a pyramid that had been drawn on a board. As the pyramid went higher it skipped from event to event until finally, at the top, sat a name. 'Sonny Pike'. It was their plan, I was told, to turn me into the Coca-Cola Kid. It had a ring to it, I'll give them that.

Joining Coca-Cola in using me as a way of shifting healthy, wholesome nutrition was McDonald's. In addition to featuring in advertising campaigns, the pair of them had me attend corporate events. There, I'd be expected to juggle the ball in the air and wow the onlooking suits. I must have done all right because after a few events Coca-Cola asked me to perform at the Coca-Cola League Cup final that season, which was taking place at the home of English football: Wembley.

I was overawed at the prospect and began seriously juggling straight away. Terry would often get me to do keepie-uppies to work on my control, but with four weeks' notice until my Wembley appearance I practised like crazy. I went down the park and asked my mates to count for me. From getting hundreds I was soon getting thousands. With less than a week until my big day I was practising over at the park near Dad's Green Street flat by Enfield Lock. I managed to track down a mate to count for me, but as the ball carried on bouncing off my feet and remaining in the air I could feel him getting bored and checking his watch. "Here, Sonny, I've got to go have some dinner. Can you count from now?" With the ball still in the air, another mate came over to carry on counting where he'd left off. When that first mate returned to the park from his dinner I still hadn't dropped the ball!

Wembley had always been my mecca. Ever since seeing that picture of the Enfield first team celebrating on the pitch and thinking 'that could me'. Ever since learning about what it represents, its cultural significance, the incredible players that have played on its surface. Ever since my one previous visit, to the 1992 FA Charity Shield with Dad, which ended in a 4-3 victory for Leeds United over Liverpool.

But this time it was going to be totally different.

I arrived on the morning of the final and was directed to my own special entrance by the towers, just as if I was one of the players who'd be playing in the League Cup final later that day. Inside everything was immaculate, fancier than anything I'd seen before. I was whisked from one set of suits to another, my Mizuno boot bag clutched under my arm and Dad at my side. I felt like a proper player already.

A guy with a clipboard spotted me amongst all the madness and took me on a tour of all the areas I needed to be in later. That was where I'd get changed, he pointed out. You need to be there at 1:30pm. That was the tunnel. And here's the pitch.

Wow.

The whole time the guy was writing stuff down on his

clipboard, more instructions coming into him through a combination of the headset he was wearing and all kind of different suits racing about the stadium.

Minutes before kick-off, I was ready and waiting. I put on the white shirt with red Coca-Cola branding, then the white Umbro shorts and white and red socks, which I kept rolled down. Finally, I laced up my black Mizuno boots, tongue down. I waited and waited, remaining excited for what was to come. Then the man with the clipboard appeared and all of a sudden he said I had to go, right now, and I followed him, weaving in and out of the people milling around the tunnel. Then I heard the stadium announcer saying my name out loud to the entire crowd: "Here's Sonny Pike, the Coca-Cola Kid."

Wow.

I felt like I was in the film Gladiator. There were seas of people, eyes wherever I looked – 80,000 pairs of them. It was overwhelming. I couldn't look around me. Couldn't take it all in. If I paid too much attention to the crowd I knew that nerves would get the better of me. Instead I had to do what I always did: just focus on the ball.

They'd given me a red and white Coca-Cola ball. I clutched onto it, then when I reached the centre of the pitch – just as I'd been instructed to do – I threw the ball up and started my performance. The guy with the clipboard had asked me to start with the Baggio Seven, a set of juggling skills that involved moving the ball in a semi-circle by keeping it up with the right foot, right thigh, right shoulder, head, left shoulder, left thigh then left foot. I took my first touch with my right foot, moving the ball up to my thigh. Corr, they hadn't half pumped the ball up. It's ideal to have a nice soft ball so it slaps off your thigh and loops up onto your shoulder. Little things like that would have been fine down the park, I wouldn't have thought twice about it, but on the pitch at Wembley it was totally different. The ball made it a bit harder than usual and for a split second it threw me off. But then I managed to navigate the ball onto my head and once you're halfway with the Baggio Seven the rest is easy. The hard part is getting the ball up from the thigh to the shoulder, then the shoulder to the head. Down is easier. Especially when the ball is as solid as a rock. Once I was successful with the Baggio Seven I found that I could relax. In the background I could hear people clapping and shouting my name. I'd done what I needed to. I'd carry on juggling until the guy with the clipboard told me to stop. Soon enough I lost myself in the ball's movement. When you play a game of football all background noise disappears and you just zone in on you and the ball. Everything else is secondary, and so was the case as I carried on performing for all of those people. And then it was over. The stadium announcer announced my name once more, Sonny Pike: the Coca-Cola Kid and finally, finally, I was able to look around me and properly take in the sea of faces applauding me. I'd never known such a buzz.

I walked off the pitch and back down the tunnel as if in a daydream, absolutely buzzing, a complete bundle of emotions. The guy with the clipboard was marching quickly but I noticed the Aston Villa and Leeds United players were starting to line up in the tunnel and held back, lingering as best I could. I wanted to see if Aston Villa striker Dwight Yorke was wearing the gold pair of boots that had been given only to the two of us. He wasn't, but he was wearing the same black and white pair that I had on, which was more than enough for me.

With my performance safely done, I was then invited to watch the final thanks to the two complementary tickets Coca-Cola had given me. Dad had other plans, though. Before we'd gone into the stadium that morning he'd tried to sell the two tickets for £200 a pop! Fortunately, he was unsuccessful, and 10 minutes into the game I settled into my posh Wembley seat and watched until the 80th minute, then headed back into the corporate rooms of the stadium. I was given a fresh pizza out of a box and watched on a TV screen as Yorke added Villa's third goal to put the gloss on his team's performance. After the final whistle, I was given my ball again and carried on from where I left off before kick-off, juggling for all of the corporate suits for the next few hours. When I left I received my own gloss on the day – a whole heap of Coca-Cola merchandise such as water bottles, balls and goals.

The next day I marched down to the park with my big zip-up Coca-Cola bags like a legend. We'd never had proper goals at the park before, always using the chain link fence or jumpers for goalposts. As soon as I unzipped my new Coca-Cola goals the kids came running. I handed out red water bottles and footballs and they went mad. As far as they were concerned, that was the greatest thing I'd done.

Yet even greater things were to come. I don't know if it was because of the amount of attention I was getting from the media and sponsors or whether it really was down to my ability on the pitch but, as part of football's new-found obsession with showbusiness and glamour, Sky Sports decided to create their own awards ceremony. The biggest names in the game were set to be honoured and I too was due to receive an award at their swanky London event. Schools Champion, it was called, and to be honest I'm not sure they even considered giving it to anyone else.

As soon as the news became common knowledge there was a message from the fashion designer Paul Smith. He wanted me to model some of his new range alongside the band Supergrass and also to create a bespoke suit for me to wear at the event, and he invited our whole family down to Covent Garden to meet him. When we arrived at his flagship store we realised that this wasn't any old meeting. There was music blaring, food and drink laid on, and the place was rammed with famous people like Samuel L Jackson, all celebrating his 50th birthday. It wasn't long before he clocked me and the rest of my family and he waded through his guests to greet us, which was just as well because I didn't have a clue who he was. I'd heard of his clothes but never knew what he looked like.

"Come with me, Sonny," he gestured, leading me behind this great big glass counter. He got a key and opened up the back. "Take whatever you want, take whatever you want," he insisted, shoving handfuls of toothbrushes and other small bits of memorabilia with Paul Smith's name on them. I didn't have a clue what to do so I just stood there with about 20 toothbrushes in my arms, smiling and saying thank you.

I came away from Paul Smith's party dead impressed. He was obviously an important person but he had so much time for me. He dressed a little whackily, his grey hair all over the place and his clothes colourful, but he was so down to earth. Proper normal. Dad seemed just as impressed and the next week we went back to the store, where we were taken downstairs to have a custom cream suit fitted. With all of the mainstream media set to attend Sky Sports' awards ceremony, Dad insisted that I look the part. And I did. I felt smart in my new suit, which was just as well because I'd been told that there were more than 7,000 people with tickets to the event. I'd won awards before of course, but nothing like this. This was different.

We were picked up from Willow Road by chauffeur in a brand new, blacked out, stretched Mercedes that looked more like a limousine. That was certainly different. Even Dad was impressed. "Oh my God, look at this car they've got you!" he exclaimed. Mum and my sisters were so excited. So was my mate Andy, a team-mate at Charlden Youth who had become a close friend after moving from Edmonton to Enfield and would be part of my official party for the evening.

After arriving at London Arena an official-looking man shuttled me backstage, where I was to remain until being called out to collect my award. Dad often said that I was so laid-back I was almost horizontal but on this occasion that couldn't have been further from the truth. My heart was racing. As the place filled up I looked out and there they all were. My idols. Alex Ferguson, Alan Shearer, Paul Gascoigne, the icons of the game.

Fortunately, I was in good company backstage. The boxing star Prince Naseem Hamed, actress Danniella Westbrook and television presenter and DJ Chris Evans all took turns to speak to me as we waited for my moment. Another boxing legend, Chris Eubank, was walking around with his monocle on, which Dad agreed was probably a bit much. All of the awards were lined up to the side of us and Chris Evans led me over to the biggest one, grabbing it and stuffing it under my jacket. "You can have that one," he joked, and when I tried to pull it out to put it back on the table he only held it tighter, so it stayed in my bespoke cream Paul Smith jacket. Eventually I managed to put the award back in its rightful place, casting my eye over all of the others. They were majestic. Back then I thought that they were all solid gold. Pure, solid, 32-carat gold.

I was having such a good time that all of my nerves had left me. It didn't matter that the show was over-running and we'd missed our slot. After all, my award was just a filler between two of the main awards and could be done at any time. Not that Danniella, who was due to present it, felt the same. "We should have been on half an hour ago!" she moaned. "What are they playing at? Get somebody over here, I want this sorted." I ignored her frustrations. Other people's presentations had been delayed and they were being as good as gold. What made me more important? Even Dad was shaking his head at her. Despite her outbursts, I was feeling calm and comfortable amongst my new friends. But then Dad's latest brainwave hit him.

"Here, son", he said. "I want you to put these up your sleeve, then when you receive your award get them out and wave them about."

Once Dad has an idea in his head there's no stopping him. I reached out and grudgingly accepted his two small Union Jack flags on plastic poles. I really didn't want to wave them about. I wanted to go on stage and not mess up. Just get my award and say my thank yous. I didn't want to have to add the pressure of waving about those flags.

But there was no time to argue. After waiting for so long, I received my cue and walked out into the bright lights and the applause of 7,000 people.

A smiling Ian Wright, stood alongside Danniella, handed me my award and it was a great feeling. Somewhere out there Alex Ferguson – Alex Ferguson! – would have been applauding me. I said a couple of thank yous in a pretty brief speech, got another round of applause, and then reached into my sleeve. I pulled and out came the plastic poles. And that was all. The Union Jacks were stuck somewhere up my sleeves. Rooted to the spot, I didn't know what to do. There were 7,000 pairs of eyes looking at me, a 12-year-old kid sheepishly holding two plastic poles. There was no time to correct the mistake. Even if I dived into my sleeve there'd be nothing to wave the flags with.

Cutting my losses I walked off the stage, award in hand, all the while not feeling happy that I'd been given such a prestigious award, but disappointed that I'd let my dad down.

As soon as I was backstage I was bundled into a press room where all of the award winners were lined up. Everything was a blur as some savvy photographers ushered me down into a seat next to George Best, who'd been inducted into the Sky Sports Hall of Fame. There I was, the 'new George Best', next to the original. It was a comparison I welcomed. I'd seen all of the tapes of him in action and thought he was a true legend. We both had the same style of play, going off on mazy runs at regular intervals in the 90 minutes. I love it when players have a licence to do their own thing on the pitch. It makes for the best kind of football. As I sat down George leaned over, putting his arm around me. "Nice to meet you, Sonny," he said. "Hope you do well." Even though I was only a kid I could tell he was drunk. He meant what he said and he was smiling and laughing but it was obvious he wasn't sober. For starters he had his award the wrong way round, so I leant over him and turned it so that it was facing the right way for the photographers. I didn't think it was that funny but all the photographers started laughing so I felt like I had to give them a smile.

Still there were more photographs, cameras constantly flashing in my direction. "Don't worry about them, just stay with me and I'll look after you." It was Ian Wright, who'd made his way over and appeared at my side. It was as if the Arsenal striker knew what I was thinking and he instantly put me at ease. In his brown chequered suit he stood out from anywhere in the room. I'd always be able to find him.

But until I was comfortable in my new surroundings he didn't let me out of his sight. He was a proper gentleman, really genuine, and asked me all about the team I played for, my position, my training schedule and school. It was best to skip over that last question.

Once the photographers had all of their shots the music came on and the drinks started flowing. We were free to mingle, and Dad wasted no time in heading over to the boxers. You know that film quote – "I could'a been a contender"? Terry looked pretty satisfied to still be talking to Ronnie Wood from The Rolling Stones after they'd watched the awards ceremony together, and to keep me company I had Ian Wright, who seemed intent on making sure I was enjoying myself throughout the night.

"Hello Terry!" I said, waving my award at him.

"Here Sonny," Terry replied. "I'd like to introduce you to Mr Wood from the Rolling Stones."

"Oh yeah?" I smiled at Mr Wood briefly. "Where's Mum?"

"I'm sorry Mr Wood," Terry said to his new friend. "He'd be going crazy if you were Oasis."

Then, suddenly, someone was going crazy because of Oasis. In the middle of the room there was a big commotion. The cameras were out in force and they were all pointing in one direction: my dad. There he was, squaring up to Liam Gallagher, who had been walking around and giving it the big 'un since the party began. His behaviour had been grating on my dad and eventually it proved too much.

"Why are you such an arsehole?" Dad scowled from inside the hordes of paparazzi, loud enough to divert everyone's attention and put Liam Gallagher off his stride. Dad held his look, glaring straight into Liam Gallagher's Brit Pop façade. I knew what that look meant. One more flash of arrogance and he wouldn't think twice about chinning him. I was absolutely shocked. What was Dad saying that for? I didn't know what to do and so all that I could do was watch as the scene unfolded before my eyes. Liam Gallagher was looking back into my dad's eyes, challenging him.

"You know why I'm an arsehole?" he asked, pausing ever so slightly, as if he was inviting my dad to answer back. "Because I'm fuckin' rich." That shut Dad up. Soon enough he was back over with his boxers, Liam Gallagher had moved on and the pack of photographers had dispersed.

Ian Wright was by my side and later we were joined by Sylvester Stallone. "Hey kid, you look like a real athlete," he said as we posed for a photograph together. Then Prince Naseem came up to me. "I've heard all about you, Sonny," he said, picking me up and shaking my hand. "Your old man says you reckon you're better at football than I am at boxing." My heart stopped. I'd never said anything like that. Why was he making up such things? Prince Naseem loved it though. He possibly revelled in his own arrogance and my false words seemed to enthuse him. Do this, do that and you can be this, he was telling me, eagerly laying out my future career path before insisting that we mucked around with some shadow boxing.

The rest of the night passed without incident and before long we were told our cars were ready. They'd got us all these big limousine-type Mercedes for the journey home, and I got in ours with Mum, Dad and Andy. The best bit about the car was that it had two seats at the rear which faced backwards, so me and Andy plonked ourselves down in those. Exhausted, I was looking out of the window at the insatiable press taking their pictures when there was an excitable tug on my sleeve.

"Look Sonny, it's Ian Walker!" Andy exclaimed, pointing at the car behind us. He was right. Tottenham's goalkeeper was in the car behind us and we were facing straight at him. "Ian!" we both screamed, frantically waving at the curtain-haired man in front of us. We caught his attention and he was looking at us. But he wasn't waving. We waved harder, screaming even louder. Ian! Ian! Aware that he should probably do something, Ian Walker slowly raised his hand, but rather than give us both a wave he merely stuck his middle finger up. Brilliant! Ian Walker was giving us the finger. It was amazing and we both stuck our fingers up back at him, all the while laughing hysterically.

Soon enough our car turned the corner and we were gobbled up into London's relentless traffic. As our Mercedes travelled along I stared into the bright lights from outside, delighting in how they illuminated the golden award that sat proudly on my lap. I touched it to make sure it was real. Even with it on my lap I still couldn't believe that this had all happened. Why me? That was the overwhelming question going around in my head. Why me? How has it come to this?

I knew I was beyond lucky. I was a 12-year-old kid from Enfield and yet I had everything a professional footballer had – more, in fact. Everything had all started to kick off with the Premier League and Sky TV and here I was, cannoned right to the front of the boom and reaping the rewards. A boot deal with Mizuno? Sponsorship from Paul Smith? It was the kind of thing most professional footballers dream about. I wasn't picking up a salary from a professional club but there were plenty of organisations paying handsomely to have me on board. As I sat back and clutched my award I couldn't help the recurring thought that was whirring around my head: 'I've got it all already,' it said. 'What else is there left to do?'

9: Great Exploitations

"Remember to tell them that you don't like the way football is played in England and you much prefer it abroad. Oh, and make sure the camera sees that Ajax badge."

It was always the same pep talk before the cameras started rolling. At first I argued that we shouldn't say bad things about the English game, but eventually I learned to just nod and accept what he said. Dad had learned the power that came from saying I preferred football abroad. He'd seen the media lap it up and so every interview became a case of regurgitating his words. I never found that I could relax until I'd said what my dad had told me to say. I was petrified of messing up. I was scared of letting him down. When you know what your dad is capable of, when you've felt the full extent of his aggression, you make sure you do what he says. If not you could be at the wrong end of a clip round the ear. Or a knee to the face.

"You've just got to say it a few more times then you don't have to say it anymore," Dad would often assure me. But then the vicious cycle we were trapped in would whir. One brand would see that I was working with another and ask me to come on board. One interview would lead to 10 more. There were always more people, more opportunities, but always the same questions, always about Ajax, Ajax, Ajax, which meant I always had to say the same thing. A few times turned into hundreds of times. Sometimes the pressure of repeating Dad's words meant I forgot to make other important points; other times it was far worse.

We always did the interviews at Mum's house in Willow Road to give the impression we were a proper family. The journalists came in their droves. At first it was fine, but little more than a couple of weeks after my Dutch experience I got absolutely sick of talking about Ajax. What was the point in talking about Ajax when I could be playing football? The sickness combined with the anxiety and together they proved overwhelming.

One afternoon I looked down from my bedroom window to see yet another camera crew knocking at the door. Another one? My mind cast back to the flight home from Ajax, telling Dad I was looking forward to getting back to football, Dad agreeing. I felt cheated. Suddenly it all felt wrong. Too much. Dad always told me that every interview would be my last, but they kept on coming. As he answered the door and the crew stepped into the house I lost it. The anxiety was too much. Tears flooded down my face as I struggled for breath. It was a full-blown panic attack. Dad called for me to come down but I couldn't answer. I couldn't do anything except move into the hallway. Wondering what was going on, Dad left the crew in the living room and came upstairs. What he saw surprised him to say the least. He quickened his pace and pushed me back into the room so none of the camera crew could see the state of me or hear my sobs. With his palm on my chest, I just about managed to get some words out. "Dad, I don't want to do this." I backed away from his palm, backing all the way to my bedroom. Still Dad came with his palm out. Still I backed away, all the way until the wall and suddenly I could back away no more. There was nowhere left to go. I crumpled onto the bed, still in fits of tears. I breathed shallow breaths, trying as much as I could to get air into my lungs. Dad simply sat down next to me on the bed and put his arm round me. The anxiety calmed. Breaths came easier. I breathed deeper, deeper again. The sobs became tears, then eventually stopped. Dad was with me. I no longer felt scared. I was safe. Dad talked softly through everything. He told me it would all be fine and it was going to be an easy interview. Then he repeated the line that he'd already repeated so often. "It's just a few more times then you don't say it anymore."

He said it with such authority that in that moment I believed him.

After half-an-hour waiting in the living room of Willow Road, the camera crew must have been left scratching their heads. Had they got the wrong day? The wrong house? But eventually they saw me. I calmed myself sufficiently and then mustered up enough energy to go downstairs and present myself as Sonny Pike: Superstar, rather than Sonny Pike: Overwhelmed by Anxiety. Sonny Pike: Superstar spoke freely about how he didn't like English football and how football abroad is much more skilful. Sonny Pike: Superstar repeated all of his dad's words and made sure that the camera crew left fully satisfied. Sonny Pike: Overwhelmed by Anxiety hated every second of the whole act he was putting on and couldn't wait for the adults around him to leave, but nor could he bear to let his father down.

The damage had been done. I'd had the first panic attack of my life. As I was about to find out, it would be far from my last.

When you're constantly hyped up as the next big thing, you become under increasing pressure. Wherever you go, people watch on. Yet more hype meant more interviews, which meant less time training. And still I was expected to produce. At times it felt like I was drowning.

"Sonny trains for up to 30 hours a week with school or county teams, as well as with his personal coach, Terry Welch," *The Young Daily Telegraph* reported, "But Sonny still manages to squeeze school-work into his punishing schedule."

Punishing schedule. They got that one right. Yet despite the requests and the instructions and the inability to focus solely on football, the key elements of my game were still there. I had no problems in scoring at will. Even with all of the rough treatment I was getting on the pitch, the cries of "take him out!" and "break his legs!" that only got louder with every media appearance I made. And I didn't even have to be playing football to have people threatening me.

I could just be on the swings down at the park and have people shouting at me. Sometimes they were much older than me. One kid in particular gave me a hard time. He was the same age as Dominique, five years older than me, and used to often mouth off at me. "You're no good, Sonny! Watch me break your legs, it won't matter anyway." That was until my sister caught wind of what he was doing. While he was mouthing off at me, she moved up behind him and put her finger to her lips, urging me to be silent. When she was within reach she tapped him on the shoulder, then when he turned there was a loud crack. She lamped him right round the mouth! Dominique always was a bit of a wild one. I had to jump off the swing and stop her from causing real damage. The boy emerged from the tangle of bodies with a bleeding lip, urging me to make my sister leave him alone.

The sixth sense I developed on the pitch to keep me away from rash challenges soon became useful in other settings. Kids from places a little further afield than Enfield, who only saw me on the TV and in the papers and thought that I was a big-time Charlie, saw me as a new target. The first time I learned of it, I was in the Odeon cinema right at the bottom of Willow Road watching *Running Man* with my mates. The five of us were buzzing, feeling properly grown up because we were still 12 years old and not officially old enough to be watching the film. The opening credits played and we all settled down in total satisfaction. Until my mate Steven needed the toilet. Soon enough he was weaving his way past people in the dark. "Excuse me, excuse me." When he came back, though, he was noticeably shocked. "Sonny," he said and straight away I was thinking fucking hell, what's going on here? I could tell something wasn't right. "There are some people outside. They're all from Edmonton and they want you outside right now. They reckon they're going to beat you up."

I'd never felt fear like it.

I was glad it was dark in that cinema because my face must have been a picture. My whole body froze up instantly; a dead weight. My mouth remained wide open. Even if I had wanted to get up and go outside it wouldn't physically have been possible. Nothing like that had ever happened before. This wasn't some opposing player desperate to win a game of football and coming in with a vicious slide tackle. This was proper, pre-meditated violence that had no real purpose other than bragging rights. I could imagine the kids now, going back to their mates in Edmonton saying, 'Guess what? We beat up Sonny Pike. Taught him a lesson.'

Why would anybody want to do that?

I couldn't concentrate for the rest of the film. Every scene was a scene closer to my inevitable beating from the Edmonton kids. The thought of them, of even going out of the cinema, filled me with dread. My mates didn't look too sharp about it either. As the end credits rolled and the cinema lights came on, we didn't have much choice. Cautiously, we headed to the exit and pushed the doors open. Stopped. Looked left and right. Nobody. They had to be there. They weren't: the coast was clear. Together we left the cinema and emerged into the outside world. Five 12-year-old kids, all of them feeling a massive sense of relief. We said our goodbyes on the corner of Willow Road. My mates all went in their different directions to their houses. All I had to do was get back up Willow Road. A five-minute walk, that was all it was. Then I'd be safe in my mum's house where nobody could get me. I quickened my pace, keeping my wits about me. Three minutes. Nothing. Four minutes. I'd made it to Aldersbrook Park. Almost home. "Sonny!" two of my mates from school spotted me and ran across the road. "Sonny!" I stopped and acknowledged them. Breathlessly, they told me information that made my blood run cold. "There are 20 kids over there and they're after you. They want to beat you up." The Edmonton gang must have gone from the cinema to the park to wait for me. How did they know where I hung out, where I lived? I turned to look at where my two schoolmates were gesturing, then I saw them. Even worse, they could see me. There really were about 20 of them. And only one of me. Immediately, they started coming towards me. "Run, Sonny!" my schoolmates urged me. I wanted to run, but at the same time I didn't want to show them that they'd got to me. No, I couldn't let them see me running. I'd just turn and walk back to my house. I might just about be able to make it. I could hear their footsteps and their cries but I was closing in on my house. All I had to do was cross the road and I'd be home. Safe. I took one step off the pavement and – bang! I was down. The first Edmonton kid had reached me and given me a right hander to the side of my mouth. I'd fallen forward into the road. A car swerved around my motionless body and then they were all on me.

I looked up and they were all there, blocking my vision. But that was all they did. They stared me out but left me to pick myself up. They left me as I got to my front door and they left me as I went inside.

They had what they'd come for: they could go back to Edmonton and boast that they'd bashed up Sonny Pike. Taught him a lesson. He needed it teaching anyway. He was shit at football.

Mum clocked straight away that I was shaken up. When I told her what had happened she was on the phone to her brother before I could finish the story. Moments later, Uncle Victor appeared in his white van. "Get in," he told me. We drove off in search of the Edmonton kids. Uncle Victor was a normal bloke, a painter and decorator who provided service with a smile, but what had happened had riled him up. He was determined to find them. They weren't at the park anymore. They weren't by the cinema either. Still, Victor carried on driving. And then we spotted them. I pointed them out to Victor and he jumped out of the car, drawing himself to his full height. "Listen you kids, if this ever happens again there will be trouble."

That told them.

A few days later I spotted them again. This time they were loitering around the entrance to the park. I was with Terry, the pair of us planning to do a one-to-one training session in the park. There was no option but to walk past them. Yet when we did, they merely parted and let us through. Terry could tell that something was up. He knew I'd been roughed up a few days before. It was only in the break of our session that I let him know it was those same kids, though, and by that time they were gone.

Yet no sooner had the Edmonton kids gone then the Tottenham kids came for me. In Tottenham I was known as someone who kicked about on the artificial turf behind White Hart Lane, but nobody there really knew me as a person. I liked to go and test myself by playing on the streets and in the parks with kids further afield than Enfield to see what the standard was like. Tottenham was one of those places and, together with Roy, I'd go down there semi-regularly and get involved. One day we were playing until late, losing ourselves in the game as always, when all of a sudden we realised we were the only people left. Another two fellas came up to me and said "Sonny Pike?" as people often did.

"Yeah, yeah," I replied. "That's me."

"We've heard of you. What are the girls like in Enfield?"

"Yeah, they're all right. They're nice."

And then there were a whole load more than just the two. A big gang of kids came over looking for trouble. Like the two before, they started with "Sonny Pike?" but unlike the two before, they weren't interested in life in Enfield. They were threatening, after trouble. Another gang who wanted to give it the big 'un that they'd bashed up Sonny Pike. Me and Roy prepared for the worst but it didn't come. The first two who came over stood up for us. They pleaded my case and managed to defuse things. For a while.

The next week I was in my maths class at Chace Community, which was rare enough given the circumstances, when news got round that a gang of Tottenham kids had broken into the school and were running around the classes demanding to know where Sonny Pike was. 'Fucking hell, what's going on here? These Tottenham kids are next level,' I thought, once again frozen to my chair. Fortunately, frozen to my chair was where I remained. The Tottenham kids were escorted off the Chace premises and never came back. I soon learned that I had to watch myself at all times.

Some of the more unwelcome attention came from more covert sources. Anonymous messages were spray painted on the alley walls around Willow Road saying *Sonny Pike is shit*. Mum's car got smashed up. Letters were posted to my mum's house from a middle-aged woman saying all of the filthy things she'd like to do to me. They were the most terrifying thing of all.

JEALOUSY REARS ITS UGLY HEAD, yelled *The Enfield Advertiser* in response, ***ANOTHER BIG EXCLUSIVE: HOW FAME IS PROVING HARD TO HANDLE FOR ENFIELD'S CHILD PRODIGY***, before telling of the vandalism and messages.

After all the months of non-stop attention following Ajax I was wiped out, both physically and mentally. Mum noticed the change in me and asked Terry if he could watch out for me. She was concerned Dad was working me too hard and Terry agreed. He referred to all of my interviews and brand deals as "the nonsense". From that moment, Terry became part of the furniture at Mum's house. He'd always call in before our training sessions so he could walk our dog. Afterwards, he'd chat with Mum and they got to know each other well. Terry would then accompany me on more of my shoots. Dad was happy to have him along. With Terry on the scene we looked like a right professional outfit: Dad, son and personal coach in front of the cameras.

Terry had no problems with fighting my corner but his voice was often drowned out by all around him.

When he was allowed to speak, he spoke freely, as in my *Hello!* magazine interview.

"I believe in him totally," Terry says. "As adults, if we see such talent it's our responsibility to encourage it now, not later when it's too late. You can teach many things but you can't teach experience.

"I'm always hearing stories about young boys who had potential and now spend all their time down the pub. Why? Because we didn't look after them when it mattered. The guardians of the game are asleep on guard."

Terry empowered me to question more of my dad's decisions, but my voice similarly ended up being drowned out. There was the time I wasn't allowed to play in the final of a tournament at Butlins because I was invited on to a breakfast show the following morning. My sixth sense had already been put into action by that point when a group of kids recognised me out the front of the chalet I was staying in doing keepie-uppies. They approached me and I knew straight away they were after a fight. I'd seen it enough times to know by then. I turned and ran, feeling their footsteps hot on my heels. I turned the corner and there was Mark Coles, our assistant manager at Charlden. I'd never been more relieved to see him. Mark was only five years older than us but we all thought he was properly cool. He had the curtains haircut with an undercut and always wore one of those big, baggy Umbro jumpers. "Oi!" he spotted the kids chasing me and clocked what was going on. "Leave him alone!"

When you're 12 and get threatened by a 17-year-old, you do what the 17-year-old says.

That whole week had been red hot and there were a few tired players on the eve of the final. My dad had received the phone call inviting me onto *Big Breakfast* that afternoon, and there had been a request for some of my team-mates to join. I didn't even want to go myself. I wanted to play football, just as I always did. I wanted to win the final for my mates. But I had no choice. I had to do what Dad wanted. The others had a choice. There was a big debate that evening about the right thing to do. Parents and kids met in the middle of the chalets. Half were up for it, the other half were outraged. "You can't leave the team!" they appealed. The outraged got their way. Some of my team-mates still fancied it, but the next morning I left Butlins at the crack of dawn, alone except for my dad. While I was in the *Big Breakfast* garden doing keepie-uppies with Sharon Davies, they were preparing to take part in the final. Just as I should have been.

The questions kept on coming. Why was I having to miss so much football when I was supposed to be a footballer? Why was I still missing so much school when I was supposed to be in school?

Then, one of the worst occasions that really had me

questioning what was going on: a McDonald's advert shot over in west London by the QPR training ground. The director had me on an artificial pitch doing the Baggio Seven, the same set of juggling skills that I'd performed on the hallowed turf at Wembley Stadium in front of 80,000 people. This time was different, though. I hadn't been looking forward to it for weeks. There was no excitement attached. It was just another job. Not one for which I'd been training for weeks. I'd even been training that very morning, but not for the advert. Instead, I was training with Terry, training to make myself a better footballer. With time tight, I'd had to skip lunch. I hadn't eaten before the shoot and planned to grab some food before the cameras started rolling. The crew didn't know that, and for them time was tight too. I begged Dad to get me some food but he was adamant: I had a job to do. And anyway, I wasn't allowed any food while on set. So I set about doing the Baggio Seven over and over again, my stomach rumbling with every kick, energy leaving me at every moment. Right foot, right thigh, shoulder, dropped. Try again. Right foot, right thigh, right foot. That's not right. Do it again. Right foot, right thigh, shoulder, head, left shoulder, left thigh, left foot. That's right. Now do it again. And again. And again.

It was an age before the crew were happy with the shot. Far from being over, that was only the beginning. After the Baggio Seven, I was made to shoot endless volleys into a camera lens.

"My legs are killing me," I complained to Dad. "My knees are red raw. I'm starving. Can't we finish?" But Dad remained adamant. He'd always been proud of the Pikes' work ethic and nothing could alter that perception.

"You're getting paid. You're here to do a job."

There was no use in arguing. He was so forceful.

This was no longer 'the nonsense' as far as Terry was concerned.

It was Great Exploitations.

And there was nothing we could do about it.

Interlude: The Promise

SONNY IS SLY'S PRIZE GUY

Daily Express
Tuesday January 30, 1996
By Frank Malley

Sonny, real name Luke Santino Victor Michael, spent a week training at Ajax's centre of excellence last year. He scored 142 goals last season for the Chalden Youth team in Enfield and also trains at Leyton Orient.

By now you must be thinking he has a dad from hell…you know the sort – the type that made tennis star Mary Pierce's life a misery.

Sonny's dad, Mickey, is a Bethnal Green builder with an Italian wife, Stephanie, and two daughters. He said: "People might think I'm pushing him but I wanted him to be a boxer. I let him make his own decisions."

Mickey sold his car to pay for his son's trip to Denmark with England for a World Cup youth tournament. England beat

Poland 3-1 in the final, Sonny scoring twice. Not surprisingly his fame has travelled and he will entertain the crowd with his ball skills before this year's Coca-Cola Cup final. "I want to play for Ajax but I'm taking it one day at a time," says Sonny, who picked up a special Schools Champion award at London Arena in front of a 7,000 audience.

10: Monster Monster

When Chelsea came calling everything changed. This was the moment I'd been waiting for. A proper big club that I could move on to and excel at. I knew that was my level. I'd fitted in at Ajax and continued to be one of the best players in my East Anglia team.

Dad was as casual as you like when he mentioned that Chelsea had invited me over. We were just coming out of a Leyton Orient training session and he asked if it was something I'd be interested in. Interested? I could have bitten his hand off.

Chelsea were undergoing a transition as they attempted to launch themselves into the big time. Glenn Hoddle had moved on to become England manager and was replaced by Ruud Gullit, just one of a growing number of foreign stars on Chelsea's books that included my mate from Mizuno, Gianfranco Zola.

The plan was to continue training and playing once a week for Leyton Orient and carry on with East Anglia while attending Chelsea sessions. Terry questioned whether I was allowed to train with so many teams but Dad assured him that I wasn't signed on at Orient so was free to do what I wanted.

"Well if he isn't signed on then he can go anywhere. He can go to the moon if he wants, so long as he can get there," Terry replied. Terry took Dad at his word and Mum confirmed what Dad said. "He's too young for all of that nonsense," she reiterated, but she still went upstairs to double check all of my official papers.

Training at Chelsea took place in a sports hall at one of their satellite centres under the watchful eye of coach Bernie Dixon. I'd barely stepped in the front door when Bernie first introduced himself to us. "Sonny can't come here if he's signed for Orient," he announced. Terry turned to Dad, expecting him to say something, but words weren't forthcoming. Instead it was down to Terry to tell Bernie that he'd spoken to my mum, who'd confirmed that I wasn't signed on anywhere.

I was so relieved when Bernie allowed me to train and I settled in nicely. The players all welcomed me with open arms – which didn't always happen – and the coaches treated me as a normal kid. The standard, I soon found, was similar to Leyton Orient. If anything, Orient was actually better, despite their senior team being nowhere near the same standard. Chelsea was only a centre of excellence and clubs had to rely on the talent on their doorsteps rather than casting their nets far and wide. After my first few sessions Dad was getting phone calls from Bernie saying how impressed they all were with me. I felt that I was flying.

Suddenly Orient didn't seem so attractive. Neither did any of the media requests or endorsement deals. I just wanted to be left at Chelsea and allowed to concentrate on my football. But the requests kept coming. All sorts of people approached Dad with new ideas and opportunities and he lapped them up. He was constantly moving me from agent to agent, using one up for as much as possible before being suckered in by another.

And then he was suckered in by the biggest of them all. There was an opportunity to make a documentary about me, Dad was informed. It'd be presented by someone called Greg Dyke and would result in me being represented by Eric 'Monster' Hall, the biggest and most charismatic football agent of the 1990s. The offer was music to Dad's ears. Terry thought I was a bit young to have a documentary made about me but Dad reminded him about all the other documentaries that had come and gone and insisted this was "just another".

Along with Terry, we met Greg and the camera crew just outside Eric's office on Star Street, off Edgware Road. Eric, we were told, could have rented office space on any road that he wanted to. Where else, though, was more apt than a place called Star Street? It had the intended effect on Dad.

"Look at this street you're going to," Dad had told me in the car. When I saw the street name part of me thought 'oh my God'. It seemed like I was heading to some magic kind of place. But there was still that other part of me that was sick of being Sonny Pike: Superstar and missed being plain old Sonny Pike.

Dad believed the hype; I was beginning to feel burdened by it.

I didn't know who Greg Dyke was but he seemed nice. I think he was chairman of Pearson TV at the time. By that stage I'd met so many presenters and producers that he was just another grown-up. I knew all the right things to say to him. That's what practice does to you. After introducing himself, he told us all about what an important person Eric was and what we'd think about having him as an agent. I left all of that to Dad because he always dealt with that side of things, but also because I didn't really know who Eric was either. I'd been shown a photo of him before our meeting and I didn't believe that he was real. He looked just like a made-up character with his bright clothes, big cigar, "monster monster" catchphrase and distinctive features.

When we made it into his office, however, I realised that Eric certainly was real. Walking down a windy set of wooden stairs, we were shown through the open door of the basement office. There was the big cigar, the bright blue shirt, the larger-than-life personality and, of course, the catchphrase. "All right son?" he greeted me while holding his hand over the receiver of a phone. "Here, I've got someone on the line for you. It's Vinnie Jones."

Excitedly, I reached over and took the phone. "Hello?"

"All right son? How are you?" Vinnie's voice was unmistakable.

"All right."

"Now why ain't you fuckin' training?"

"I will later," I promised him.

"All right, all right."

Vinnie hung up and I passed the phone back to Eric, still unaware of just how prophetic Jones's words would be. Eric placed the phone back into its cradle and then asked Terry if he could give us some space. The office wasn't small – in fact it was quite plain, just a desk, a few chairs and a cluttered bookshelf – but he had to fit in the camera crew and Greg as well as me and Dad.

"It's a bit full in here. Would you mind going upstairs?" he asked. Terry had no other option. "There's so much room in here I could do handstands," Terry muttered on the way out. Already uncomfortable with the situation, Terry was made to wait outside while Eric played host. Eric went on to dazzle Dad with his client list, emphasising how he dealt with the vast majority of players in the Premier League and how they'd make a load of money and make me a superstar and bobbler bobbler. Eric might as well have made up a load of names for all Dad knew about football, but the whole bravado certainly impressed him. We signed off with handshakes all round and then left to relieve Terry, who was still waiting outside and growing ever more suspicious.

The next day, Eric's column in *The News of the World* told how he'd signed on Shirley Temple, a reference to the famous American child actress with long, brown curly hair just like mine. "Kids will do anything for a lollipop," he noted.

Next up a cameraman, Rick, arrived at Mum's house. That evening I was due to go and train at Chelsea and Rick wanted to get some footage before leaving. While settling in, he told me all about his work for a show called Panorama and how he'd helped uncover a big story about chicken farming.

Bernie Dixon spotted us straight away that evening. Me, Terry, Dad, and Rick were barely out of the car park by the time he marched toward us all and exclaimed "nah, nah, nah, what's that all about?" pointing toward Rick's equipment. I wanted to shrink inside myself. Already I didn't want to have a cameraman with me when I was trying to impress with my football ability and now they were making a right scene. Nobody else turned up for training with their own entourage. Dad was protesting his innocence, claiming the cameraman with his massive professional camera was there to film something for home use. It worked. Begrudgingly, Bernie allowed everyone in. Terry moved up to his usual spot in the viewing gallery above the pitch, while the others stayed on the ground floor.

The session started with a bit of passing back and forth in pairs. Boom, boom, boom, the ball moved quickly on the wooden flooring of the sports hall and my touches were feeling sharp. As always, my mind was totally on the football. Then, out the corner of my eye, I noticed this geezer's head poking up. It was the same geezer that was in my mum's living room a few hours earlier, the one with the massive camera: Rick. He had crawled underneath the green curtain that separated us off from the rest of the sports hall and was now poking his camera out from the gap, as if he were a spy. All I could see was this camera and a floating head in a sea of green. What was he doing?

With every passing second he aggravated me more and more. There was no chance I could focus on my passes. I hadn't asked for this. I hadn't asked for any of this. All I'd ever wanted was to be a footballer. And until that point, I had been closer than ever to achieving my dream. I didn't want my perfect scenario at Chelsea to be ruined. I didn't want to be on film. I just wanted to play football.

What would the other kids and coaches think?

I was sure they'd all spotted him too. With every pass the situation was becoming awkward, and thanks to the scene with Bernie before the session everyone knew who the camera was trained on.

For a good 45 minutes the camera stayed trained on me. For the final 10 minutes it disappeared but the damage had been done. My head was all over the place. At the end of the session I picked up the free Lucozade we were given and left the sports hall without saying goodbye to any team-mates, only for Dad to race over and put his arm around me like the perfect father. The cameraman was by his side, filming every second. Once they got that perfect shot, him and Dad set about laughing. They were giggling like naughty schoolboys. I couldn't figure out what had just happened. But Terry could. Walking down the stairs from his vantage point, it was immediately obvious that he had the hump. "It's not right," he insisted over and over again. "It's not right what you've done."

His words fell on deaf ears.

Terry was made to sit in the back of the car. He sulked the whole way home, cursing the Great Exploitations that were fully in motion. Dad and Rick were up in the front, talking boisterously. Once Dad had dropped Rick and Terry off and it was just the two of us he pulled the car over and made me get out. We were on some suburban street, the middle of nowhere. It was pitch black. But I followed his orders. “Don’t worry about what Terry said,” he assured me. “I’ll put him right. Don’t let him bash your ear about what you can and can’t do. You’re my son. You do what you want to do. You know I want what’s best for you. I’ll always be here for you.”

Only he wouldn’t. Because no matter how much I believed him, how much I wanted to believe him, a few weeks later he’d be gone.

11: Caught Red-Handed

"Where are we going, Dad?"

"The Orient, son. The Orient."

What? That hadn't been the plan. We were supposed to be going to Chelsea for my weekly training session. I didn't want to play for Leyton Orient, not now I was with Chelsea. But Dad was insistent.

"Stop giving me earache about going to Chelsea. I'm doing this for you." He repeated it, over and over, dragging me out of the car and speaking to me one-to-one. "I'm doing this for you. I'm doing this for you."

What else could I say?

We got back into the car and Dad started being overly nice to me. Terry was in the back watching everything. He remained silent until we pulled up to Leyton Orient's stadium.

It turned out that a game had been arranged against a touring side from the US. That's why Orient were desperate for me to play. There was, of course, another incentive for them. The TV cameras. Those same ones that had followed me to Chelsea under Greg Dyke and Eric Hall's orders were now pitching up in the stands to get the best view of the game.

Unfortunately for me, they all pitched up in the same stand. The cameras needed the best view possible of me and so I was forced to play in an unfamiliar role on the left wing. Everything I did, it seemed, was being decided by those very cameras.

Before the game, they filmed as I was introduced to Barry Hearn, the Orient chairman. He was in an expensive suit, clean shaven with slick grey hair. Greg Dyke was alongside me, as was Dad. Once again there was no room for Terry. It struck me that Barry wasn't too clued up on what was going on. Greg explained that I was a player in the youth system at Orient with great potential and Barry nodded and asked one of his staff members to fetch me a home and away kit. And that was it. Handshakes all around and then it was out onto the pitch.

The left hand side of the pitch.

Everything was the same but different. The goals were in the same place, the ball the same size, the pitch the same dimension, but everything foreign. I wanted to be up top scoring goals, not out on the left. I had this reputation as a skilful player but really that was just because I was always asked to do skills when I went on TV programmes. In reality my game was simple: get the ball and score a goal. Terry recognised the strangeness of the situation and came down from his position at the top of the stands to give me a last-minute pep talk.

"Just beat your player and get a cross in. Do that or cut inside and shoot. Use your skill."

"Is that your grandad?" A voice rang out from behind Terry. It was Barry.

"Just my football coach," I replied before darting off.

It felt reassuring with Terry there on the front row. But after that interaction the cameras asked if he could move into the back of the stands. As always Terry protested his innocence, and as always the voice of the many outweighed the lone voice. Terry had to move out of hearing. While that was going on, the action raged all around me on the pitch. My Orient team-mates hadn't been aware that the game was going to be filmed. Spurred on by the cameras, a level of intensity was added to everything they did. The ball zipped around the surface. Tackles flew in. Words were exchanged. The excitement was obvious. Amongst it all I did okay but played nowhere near as well as I knew I was capable of. Being on the left wing had really thrown me.

Yet after the game Chris Ramsey, my coach at the time, still told the cameras that I was one of the best players. There were more interviews, more handshakes and then it was all over. I was back in the car with Dad and Terry heading home.

The next few days whizzed by. Dad took me away to my grandparents' caravan in Sheerness, Kent, as a little reward. All of his brothers came along too, which meant that all of my cousins were there. It was wicked. Every year we'd go a handful of times and for those happy days I was able to live like a normal kid. We'd climb down the cliffs, go to the beach, have kickabouts and go to the clubhouse in the evenings. There was never a camera in sight.

And then the newspaper article came out.

CHELSEA TRIED TO NICK MY 12-YEAR-OLD SON: BLUES FACE RAP OVER WONDERKID
SPECIAL REPORT BY GEOFF SWEET
THE NEWS OF THE WORLD, 12 MAY 1996

It was as if Dad knew what was coming. He grabbed *The News of The World* from the small convenience shop outside the caravan site and frantically flicked through the pages before resting on the article.

"What's all this?" he exclaimed. "What's all this?" a little louder. Then louder again. I raced over to catch a glimpse of the paper. There I was, staring back out from the page, my arms wrapped around my dad's shoulders.

Chelsea face severe FA punishment after being secretly filmed making an illegal approach to soccer wonderboy Sonny Pike.

Three months BEFORE officially being allowed to speak to the hottest property in world junior football, the Premier League giants coaxed him into training with them.

And they were caught red handed, breaking a sacred code of conduct which looks certain to lead to the Blues answering Football Association charges.

"Dad," I said looking up from the paper. "This ain't good for me."

Dad didn't reply. He was frozen, his eyes still staring at

the words on the paper. Nothing he said could change what had been written though. All of those times he'd reassured me, told me I was on the right path, that he was doing what was best for me, and this was result. I was doing everything I could to play for Chelsea. But I couldn't do anything about this.

The rules on 'tapping up' youngsters – even schoolboy footballer of the year Sonny, who is tied to Leyton Orient – are hard and fast.

Until their 14th birthdays, boys are on fixed registrations and can only be approached at the end of each season.

Even then, interested clubs are supposed to write to his team and his parents, then log their request with the FA.

Instead, Chelsea allegedly chose the direct route in a bid to capture the lad from Enfield who is so good that last year he had trials with European champions Ajax.

And last night Orient chief scout Steve Shorey said: "Until now, their interest in Sonny was hearsay. I've not been able to catch them – or any other club – at it, but this seems to be the evidence I need. If it is, Leyton Orient will complain to the FA."

My heart sunk lower than low. I was absolutely gutted as I left Dad to it, traipsing back to my grandparents' caravan and collapsing in a heap on their corner sofa. Through the window I could still see my dad in the same spot, the paper still open on the same page.

He hadn't been right. Everything wasn't all right.

It hadn't all been for the best.

And I was only just starting to realise.

At the wheel: Heading into a world of adventure at Chessington in 1989

ere it all started: ceiving last-minute structions from Enfield nager Andy Kyriaku in one of first few games for a team an e group up

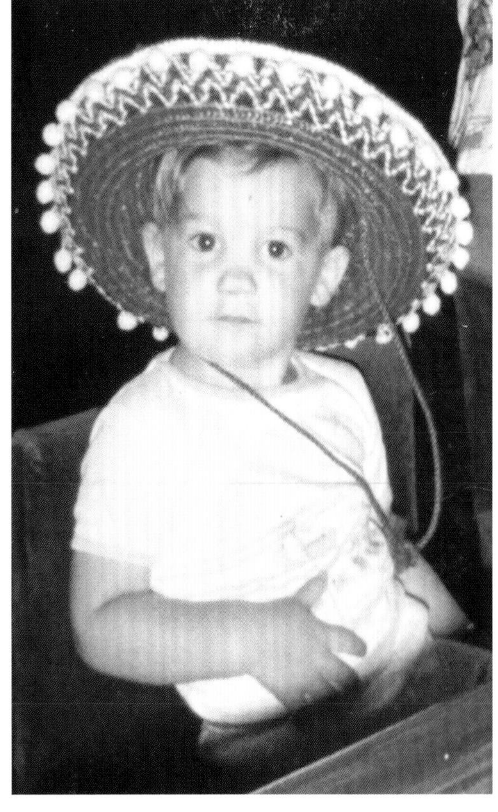

Party time in Tenerife: Early on, Mum and Dad made sure us kids had plenty of love and attention. We had some really special trips

You'll Never Walk Alone: Outside Anfield at on of the first football games I ever went to I supported Liverpool because of my primary school friend David Banfo

Magic of the Cup: Even though Spurs won the FA Cup in 1991, it didn't stop me queuing for hours to have my photo wit the trophy (the only person there wearing a Liverpool kit!)

Welcome to my playground: Sitting on Dad's car outside Enfield Football Club in the Liverpool away kit. Just out of shot lies the Starlight Rooms, where I spent many happy hours

Playing at happy families: While all looks right with the world in this image from a Hello! magazine shoot at Willow Road, the reality was that our family had been torn apart

All smiles with Terry: By this stage Mizuno were even giving tracksuits to Terry! He still looks the same age now

Show us again, Sonny: Down Aldersbrook Park with Andy Varoufakis, Patrick, Bucky and little Jimmy

Megs! We spent hours down Aldersbrook – plenty of time to perfect my dribbling

Perks of the job: In the thick of it at a Hello! magazine shoot. By this stage my room was a shrine to football with one exception: the Playboy bunny bedsheets!

In the spotlight: Picking the ties for the Subbuteo European Championships at Wembley Arena with Kenneth Wolstenholme watching on. Just out of shot is Lee Dixon

Every kid's dream: Receiving my Blue Peter badge from Tim Vincent after an Ajax session. I'd been so immersed in the training that I'd totally forgotten he was there!

New uniform day: Mizuno let me circle whatever products I wanted from their catalogue. I made the most of it!

The Pikes: Beau, Freya and Rosie are my rocks. They give me reason to wake up every day

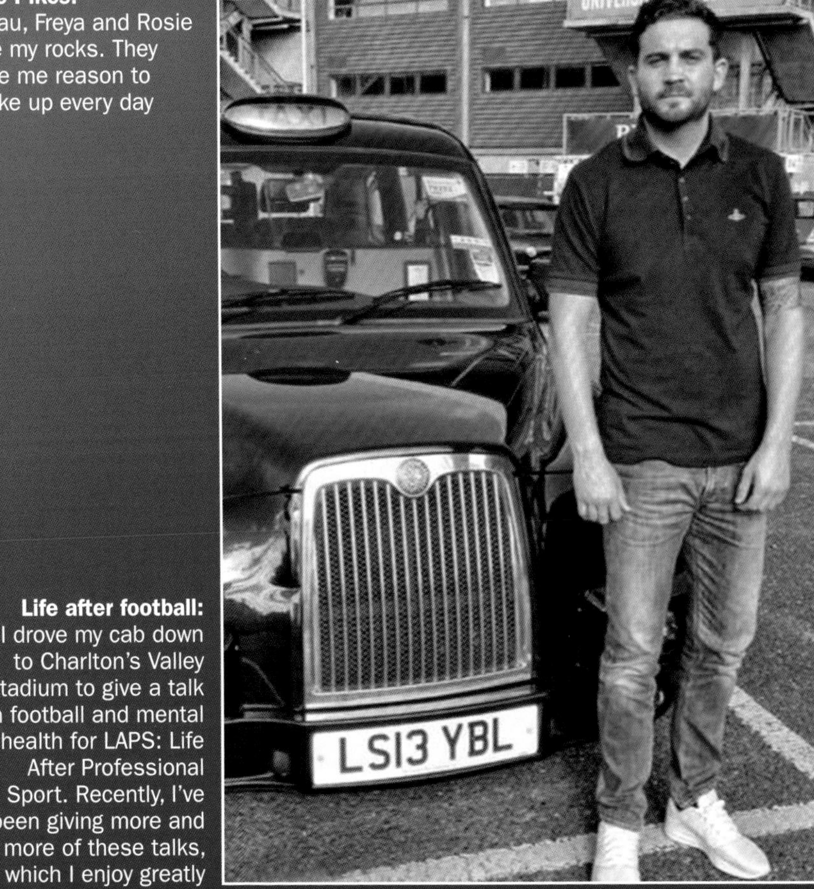

Life after football: I drove my cab down to Charlton's Valley stadium to give a talk on football and mental health for LAPS: Life After Professional Sport. Recently, I've been giving more and more of these talks, which I enjoy greatly

The future: In action at my Sonny Pike 1 on 1 Football Training academy. Here I'm talking Rudi and Jude through the importance of keeping distance between feet during a skill move

The Sky Sports 1997 awards took place later that week and once again I was to receive my own Champion of Sport award. This time was different though. I don't know if it was the newspaper article, the sheer onslaught of media appearances or the fact it was my second Sky Sports awards ceremony, but from the outset it felt less special.

Eric Hall was still representing me and managed to get me a fee of £500 for attending the awards. So far, so good. But when the day arrived it was just Dad by my side. I didn't know what to say to him. We had barely said a word to each other since the article and everything was awkward. We were picked up in a limousine and taken to the event in the London Docklands in near silence, broken only upon arrival when the paparazzi, spurred on by the *News of the World* article, were trying to lean into the car and get photos of us. We remained seated and smiled as best we could before being directed to the correct area of the venue.

This time round Sky Sports wanted me to dribble a ball onto the stage and do some passing with Andy Gray, who was hosting the night, followed by a juggling routine and then shooting at some targets in a goal.

"They're going to ask you a few questions, you know," Dad advised from backstage. "They're definitely going to ask which team you want to play for."

"I'll say Chelsea, yeah?"

"No. You tell them that they need to talk to your monster monster agent."

"But Dad, I don't want to say that!" I couldn't believe what he was suggesting. It was so embarrassing, even worse than the awards the previous year with those flags. How could I let my idols hear me saying such an outrageous thing? They were all there. Alan Shearer, Alex Ferguson, Kenny Dalglish. What would they think of me if I told Andy Gray to ask my monster monster agent? It was nerve-wracking enough being on stage, let alone having words put into my mouth.

Minutes later I jogged out onto the stage in full Mizuno kit, dribbling a ball and pulling off a few skills, just as Dad had suggested. The bright lights were all on me. The crowd's eyes were all on me. The cameras were all on me. Andy greeted me and we passed the ball back and forth while he asked questions. Every now and again I could catch a glimpse of them all. My idols, all of them seated in the front row watching on.

Jesus.

"And which team do you want to play for in the future?" The question snapped me back to reality.

"You'll have to ask my monster monster agent," I replied immediately, without even thinking.

The trust had almost gone. And yet I was still doing everything Dad asked. I cursed myself. I felt terrible. I knew I'd said what he'd told me to in an awkward manner. And suddenly the whole thing felt awkward. What was I doing here? Why was I on stage? Why was everything made to look like I had everything when in reality my world was about to fall apart?

Andy finished his segment, I performed my juggling and shooting, and then I was applauded off stage. After the ceremony there were plenty of handshakes but none of the sheer joy from the previous year. This time felt far more like a business meeting. I shook hands and greeted fellow attendees but felt sheepish the whole time as they congratulated me on my potential and told me they couldn't wait to watch me on their TV screens. None of it mattered.

The journey home was silent. Dad was next to me but he didn't feel like Dad any more. The unconditional love was eroding. Did he want what was best for me? It didn't feel like it. It hadn't for some time. He was no longer my dad; he was my manager.

12: Ruined

Everyone was looking forward to the documentary. As far as I was concerned, it was a chance to prove that everything really was all right. I was still training at Chelsea after all, and the documentary would confirm that I was a young up-and-coming player with plenty of potential. The *News of the World* article would become mere fish and chip paper. The world would move on.

Terry booked out his mate's pub in Edmonton and organised a viewing party. Invites were sent out and on the night plenty of people turned up. But one person was missing.

Dad.

It wasn't like him. He'd usually do anything he could to support my media appearances.

Terry bought me a Coke and a packet of crisps and we settled down for the evening. The big screen flickered into life and then it was on, the programme that would come to define my entire football career.

"This is Sonny Pike, one of the most sought after 12-year-olds in the country." The voiceover played over footage of me and Terry on Enfield Playing Fields, in the shadow of the first-team stadium. Both dressed head to toe in Mizuno, Terry threw balls for me to control and play back to him. "Although not allowed to sign professional forms or make money from the game until he is 17, he's already a commodity being fought over by scouts and agents in a manner that would make the cut-throat world of the adult game proud. His dad, for one, has high hopes for his career." The screen flicked to a shot of my dad sitting in my house at Willow Road with me in the background, wearing a Manchester United shirt. "He's got the skill of Pele, the strength of Cantona, the style of John Barnes – he's very stylish – and the manners of Gary Lineker." And then it was over to me. "I want to get the Golden Boot in the Premier League," I announced. But that was it. The screen changed once more, this time to Greg Dyke on the sideline of one of my games for Charlden. Greg watched on as I ran around in my oversized yellow shirt and knocked in a tap-in from a corner. Soon, though, I was no longer his main focus. Instead, he started to speak to the many scouts on the touchline. The voiceover told how scouts are controlled by a whole series of rules from the FA – or are supposed to be.

Hold on, what was going on?

This wasn't about me any more. I wasn't even on screen. This was about the scouts.

As the minutes went by I grew more and more concerned. Who were all these scouts and other kids? I thought the documentary was going to be just about me. And yet there were all these other young footballers with names like Scott Parker that I'd never heard of.

They were all shown to be like me: promising players who could have big careers in the game. Only in the documentary they weren't like me. Because the documentary was called *Fair Game: Coaching and Poaching*. They were the coaching. I was the poaching.

I was eventually shown once more on screen but there were no cheers from the watching party. There was a wariness. Looking to my left, I could see that Terry already had the hump. And it was only going to get worse.

The game from Leyton Orient played first. There was Barry Hearn, the handshakes, me dribbling down the left wing past the US touring side.

"What would you do if we told you one of these players was training at Chelsea?" Greg asked Chris Ramsey. Alarm bells started ringing in my head. Then the Chelsea footage came on screen. There I was, clear as day on the screen, passing back and forth with Bernie Dixon watching on, a flicker of curtain showing in the corner of the screen.

I stormed straight out of the pub as soon as the end credits played. I didn't even bother looking before crossing the road immediately outside the pub. I was past caring. Should I just throw myself in front of a car? I carried on walking right into the centre of the roundabout and stood there staring at the sky.

Tears.

What the fuck was going on?

I knew I was in trouble. Things had gone from bad to worse and I'd been sucked into a nightmare. Lost. Gutted. Confused. All around me the cars now circled. They seemed to be getting faster and faster until they were out of control. What could I do? All I wanted was for the world around me to slow down so I could make sense of what was going on. And instead it was doing the opposite.

In that moment I wanted Dad by my side. I needed him by my side. Not the cold, savvy, business-minded Dad, but the Dad who went out of his way to learn about the game and foster my own love of football. Where was he?

Someone approached me. They came from the shadows and picked me up and turned me round. It wasn't Dad. It was Terry. My coach. The man I knew wanted what truly was best for me. He guided me off the roundabout, past the traffic and I let him. "I need to talk to your Dad," he muttered. "That wasn't right."

I remained numb for days, unable to leave the sanctuary of my bedroom, unwilling to see anyone. Terry came to check on me regularly. Him and Mum encouraged each other on, raging against my father and Greg Dyke and Eric Hall, all of whom, in their opinion, were responsible for the state I was in. Terry was livid. Every now and again their anger would float up the stairs and into my room. Fucking Greg Dyke. Fucking Eric Hall. Fucking Murdoch press bullying whoever they want. Lying. This is a joke. It needs to be sorted.

All I wanted to do was bury myself in my bed. If I carried on sleeping then I wouldn't be awake and the reality of what had happened would go away. Who could I trust? Even though I could see that Terry and Mum were doing everything they could for me, in my paranoid mind I felt I couldn't even trust them. When awake, I thought so hard about what I could do that I gave myself headaches. Mum would often pop her head around the door to check up on me. "You okay, son?" Well, I was okay before you popped your head round the door. My head just wanted to explode. I didn't even want to see my own mother.

While Mum was worrying, Terry was on the phone non-stop to the FA, Chelsea, Leyton Orient, Greg Dyke and Eric Hall. He pleaded my case to both clubs to no avail. Chelsea had taken Orient to court and Orient had taken Chelsea to court. "Look, there's no way he can come back to Chelsea," Bernie told him. "The coaches here think the world of him, they really do, but they won't have that." Chris Ramsey said much the way. So did the FA. It'd be at least a year until I was allowed to be registered with a professional club. The damage had been done and nothing could change that. The fact was, none of us were aware that I had in fact possibly signed for Orient – that is, if a squiggle on a form at Orient that we later discovered actually did count as anything. None of us except Dad. It was his squiggle, despite the fact Mum was my legal guardian. Legally, his signature should have counted for nothing. It was just a squiggle on a page. It wouldn't have held up in a court of law. But I can see, with hindsight, why it may have looked as if I was committed to Orient. And the documentary had changed everything.

"I think that fella is mad," I told Mum on one of her visits to my room. "Terry comes round every day to do everything he can for me and I don't even speak to him. I just ignore him. But then he comes back the next day."

And come back the next day he did. Even with his progress hindered, he still had battles to fight.

"What was that crap they put on?" Terry asked when he got through to Eric.

"I don't know monster bobbler, I never watched it."

The phone rang in pain as Terry slammed the receiver down. Terry had always said he didn't blame Eric so much because he expected nothing less of agents, but still I listened in as Terry vowed that if he ever got his hands on my monster monster agent he'd end up in prison. My monster monster agent, perhaps wisely, vanished after that. So did Greg Dyke, the person that Terry pinned the most blame on.

Looking back, I question whether Greg knew the full devastating impact that documentary would have on me. From his point of view, perhaps he was just focused on making a programme about what he considered a genuine issue in the game, but at the time I saw him as someone who had brought my dreams crashing down.

Terry penned a nine-page letter of complaint about Greg and Eric to the FA. When he chased the FA up for an answer he ran into brick walls. He tried over and over again, eventually getting through.

"Listen, can I speak to someone of authority?" he raged.

"One moment please," there was a pause on the other of the phone. "Hello."

"Hello."

"Sorry, they're all out."

"What! The entire Football Association is out?"

"Yes."

"Oh right, I see. Where are they? Down Tesco?"

Terry would spend ages on the phone, trying to get the answer, any answer. Every time I heard the beeps from him dialling the FA's number I'd sit upstairs praying. Please, please, get this sorted, I'd think. I can't last much longer in limbo.

As the days became weeks, I felt more able to trust Mum and Terry. Every day I'd hear Terry come into the house with his questions: "Right, what's happening here. We're going to get this sorted. How is he then? What's he been like?"

"He ain't really come out of his room," Mum would reply.

"Well I'm not surprised. If an adult was treated that way it'd do their brains in, let alone a 12-year-old kid. But no bother, we'll get him sorted."

Terry then set about his ritual of telephoning. After a while, he'd take a break and walk Winston round the alleyways. It was on one of those walks that Dad emerged, pulling up next to Terry in his car.

"Here, Tel," he said. "You don't want to mess with them out there. You won't get nothing."

"I don't want nothing! I'm a football coach. Go and tell them that!" Terry responded, ducking into an alleyway as my dad drove off. But there was no hiding from what had happened, even in the alleyway. The graffiti had returned. *Sonny Pike is shit. Sonny pimped out by his dad.* It was there on Terry's dog walking route, at the park, in the alleyway by Mum's house, next to Chace school.

When Terry went out to walk Winston, I'd work up the courage to come out of my room. When I'd managed to do that and nothing terrible had happened, I went out of my room when Terry was in the house.

"How are you then, boy?" he'd ask as if nothing had happened. "You see the match last night?"

"Not really, I was in my room."

"We'll sort this out."

"Whatever."

Then I'd be back up to my room.

Every day I spent a little more time in his company. His consistency had rebuilt the trust. Terry wasn't like all of the other people that circled around me. He wasn't getting anything out of fighting my corner. If anything, it was costing him money. He'd never charged for one of my sessions he put on. All of the money he made from painting and decorating was put back into his football coaching. Yes, Terry was there to help me. And over those weeks in my room I had realised that I couldn't help myself alone.

I went downstairs more regularly. Then even ventured outside. But when I went outside I saw the graffiti, I felt the eyes on me. It was as if the world was mocking me.

Terry made another breakthrough when he convinced me to carry on with the one-to-one coaching. "We'll get this sorted," he said over and over. There was even a new promise. Terry would do everything he could to find me "a nice little club". "Don't worry about it, you can just go over there and be happy." I put in the hours with Terry but I found myself going through the motions. My heart wasn't in it. I was in bits, totally broken, and not even football could put me back together. What was the point? What was the point in anything?

Terry was as good as his word and got me involved at a nice little Sunday league club in Essex called Loughton. In my first training session over at Roding Valley High School I walked over to join my new team-mates on the artificial turf only to see them all nudging each other. What's *he* doing here? They were open mouthed. "It's Sonny Pike," one gasped. Throughout that session they were in my ear, constantly asking what I was doing there. I couldn't escape it. I replied to them all but found that I couldn't pay much attention to what was going on. My mind was barely even on the football.

Is Dad watching?

Is anyone filming?

Will more stories come out?

They're going to recognise me.

Do I even want to be here?

I'd never been paranoid before. Certainly not on a football pitch. I usually just went out and played football. This was different. The football was still there but now all of those thoughts were creeping into my head and refusing to go away, causing havoc. It was impossible to play my natural game. It was impossible to do anything but constantly survey all that was around me for all of the fear in my head.

One week went past. Then two. Three.

Still there was no sign of Dad. I returned to my bed, bunking off from school to just sit in my room and do nothing. The teachers there wouldn't know any different. They'd just think I was shooting a commercial or doing a TV appearance. And anyway, there was no point in doing anything else. I didn't have football and wasn't much good at anything else. My room was an environment I could control, the only place where things made sense.

The world was at my feet and then the world got taken away.

My friends came to visit me regularly. My best mate Gary was always amongst them. He'd sit on the edge of my bed and ask if I was all right and then tell me about the pirate radio station he had set up, SubJam. He'd hand over some sweets and I'd take them while still staring aimlessly at the TV. I wasn't all right. I was far from it. I was really struggling.

For six weeks I stayed holed up in my room, just about making it downstairs every now and again. On those rare times I was able to venture outside people would come up to me with smiles thinking that everything was rosy. To them I was still the kid with everything. I used to look at them and think they hadn't got a clue. It didn't matter how things looked from the outside; on the inside I'd never been in a worse way. And yet I never had the balls to tell anyone. Not Gary. Not Terry. Not even my mum. I'd have felt too embarrassed. How could anyone go from having everything to nothing?

I was nicknamed 'the king of resting' by my mates. They thought it was a bit of a laugh that I was in bed so much and I couldn't blame them. Mental health awareness was low, something still considered taboo. As I barricaded myself into the loft I racked my brains over and over. What could I do for the FA to take me seriously? How could I make everything right? I'd think and think and then only get more frustrated when I realised I was just a kid and there was nothing I could do. In those moments I'd catch a glimpse of myself in the mirror and feel disgusted. The figure looking back at me was useless. I hated him. I wanted to hurt him.

Fucking hell, Sonny. You're up against it here.

What can you do?

13: Can't Do It No More

I froze when I saw him. It had been just me and Terry on the playing fields of my secondary school, Terry laying out cones and serving the balls as I went through the motions, a mere shadow of my former self. A misplaced pass went out of the area, away from Terry, and as I jogged to retrieve the ball I heard a noise in the near distance. The paranoia sparked up instantly. Who's that? Is it him?

It was.

There were the tracksuit bottoms. The Reebok Classics. The unmistakeable flying jacket.

Dad looked at me from the other side of the chain fence. He was beckoning me toward him. I turned back to Terry and saw him watching on. I gestured that I was going to see what my dad had to say and Terry told me that he'd be right there if anything happened. With that he remained standing there, watching on.

Dad was still a good distance away, but now stepped around the fence and onto the pitches. With every step I took closer to him, the feelings built up.

Nerves.

Anxiety.

Wariness.

Love.

Fear.

"You all right boy?" he asked as always, as if nothing had happened, as if my life hadn't been turned upside down.

"What's going on, Dad?" I just about managed to whisper before finding my voice, stopping six feet away from him so I could keep my distance. "It's too much. It's all too much."

"Don't worry about that, son," he said with his usual authority and just for a second I believed him. "I've got to ask you a few questions."

"What?"

"Well I've got some more stuff for you."

"What?"

"Media. TV work."

That's when I knew our relationship was damaged beyond repair. It took all of my might to stop myself from swearing at my dad for the first time in my life. The front on him to come and ask that! He'd left me to suffer for the best part of a month and then turned up out of the blue to ask me to do the very thing that had put me in such a position.

"Dad, I can't do it no more," I told him. It wasn't a case of me pleading with him like it had always been up to that point. Instead, for the first time in my life, I was telling him that enough was enough. "I want to be a football player and I'm not interested in anything else."

Dad stared at me in shock. That wasn't in the script.

I'd never properly stood up to him before. He took a few seconds to weigh up the situation. And then he spoke and his words had more impact than any punch ever could.

"Well I ain't got a son no more then."

I stared back at my dad and could tell that he meant every single word. It was all real, and that's what made it all the more heartbreaking. Devastating. He looked at me as cold as ice and it made me feel sick. My whole throat froze. I swallowed and just about managed to get some words out.

"Well, looks like I ain't got a dad then." With that I turned and walked back to Terry, not once looking back over my shoulder at Dad. Tears fell down my cheeks. I was crying, but not uncontrollably. They were tiny, falling rather than flowing. After everything that had happened over the last couple of months I no longer had the power of emotion. I was wiped out from the constant disappointment, totally numb, left almost like a robot from the shock.

"I ain't got a fucking father no more," I announced to Terry.

"Oi! Steady you!" Terry hated it when I swore. But then I told him about what Dad had said and Terry was on the verge of swearing himself. "After all he's done!" Terry replied. "The cheek." Terry went on to tell me how he'd seen my dad spying on us during our one-to-one sessions since he'd gone into hiding, covering himself in the disguise of the trees. He'd even thrown a ball back once. Terry hadn't wanted to tell me. I was dealing with enough already.

It wasn't long until the messages started coming. A card arrived from my grandad saying "you're offside, son". The next day there was a video tape addressed to me. I popped it in and saw my dad on screen surrounded by a load of kids. "You think you're so big. You think you're too good for us, Sonny," the kids said. "But you're nothing. You're worthless." Posters went up around Enfield. Stuck over those same posters that advertised my single with Basil Simonenko that felt a lifetime ago, the new posters showed a picture of Terry with the headline: 'THIS OLD MAN IS TRYING TO SPLIT ME AND MY BOY UP.' There were no prizes for guessing who put those up.

At the same time, Dad would use Dominique, herself increasingly going off the rails following her five minutes of fame, for information on the goings-on at Willow Road. The separation had affected Dominique badly and she remained loyal to Dad, all the while getting in deeper with the wrong crowd, living the wrong kind of life, coming and going late at night and then reporting back on anything she could find.

What's Sonny up to?

Is his mum turning him against me?

Is she neglecting him?

Is he back playing football?

Has he been doing any media work, any brand deals?

Dad used parts of her information to contact the welfare office. He was that desperate to force himself back into my life. Unsurprisingly, nothing came of it. My mum always treated me well.

Dad eventually gave up. The months went by and nothing changed. He'd never be able to relive those glorious days in the spotlight and neither would I. Without him on the scene, without any agent on the scene, all of the TV and media work dried up, finally allowing me to concentrate on my football.

The year-long ban came and went. I saw it out at Loughton, which was just as Terry described, a nice little club. They had a real community feel, well organised with a nice manager, eager to get the families of players involved. There was even a dads v lads match in which my mum's new boyfriend, Joe, played. He was cut from the same cloth as my dad and slid all over the turf in his Reebok Classics. Like my dad he didn't have a clue how to play football, but his getting involved at least meant I didn't feel left out: the only kid without a dad. People went out of their way to make me feel welcome and I made a couple of good friends in the team in Ritchie and Butler. Yet even with all of that, Loughton felt like my jail: a stop-gap while I waited for the ban to run out. I played regularly, scored lots of goals, but I wasn't the same. The enjoyment was gone. I did football because I was good at it, not because I loved it. I did football because I'd need to carry on doing it after my ban. Terry would tell me how the parents on the sideline raved about me. He'd tell me that they thought I looked like a professional already. He'd tell me that scouts are always looking at what a player will be like in five years' time: faster, stronger, technical ability even higher, moving just as freely.

His words meant nothing.

In training I felt free to express myself. In matches I froze. If I pulled off an impressive skill I'd stop instantly and curse myself. It was as if I wanted to just play inside myself. To not stand out. To fit in. To ward off the aggression and the screams from the opposing parents and managers whose words no longer roared me on but frightened me. And no matter how hard I tried, the paranoia remained. Wherever I looked I imagined cameras, stories, Dad.

When my year at Loughton came to an end and the ban finished, it was the first time since I was six years old that I didn't have a club, but I felt an overwhelming sense of relief. Now aged 15, I had a chance to get back to where I was before it all went wrong. I'd be able to regain my happiness. I'd be able to enjoy football again.

My first step on the path to redemption was with a local coach called Vic Nicholls. Always decked out in an assortment of training kit from various clubs and short white socks, Vic had links with Colchester and Spurs. He ran informal training sessions for groups of talented players who were all in and out of academies.

Suddenly, I had a purpose once more, which was enough to get me out of my bed at least.

We trained weekly on the playing fields of Chace Community. Every session would start with a warm-up of sprints followed by box work where Vic would call out skills for us all to replicate. Following that we'd go into matches: never more than seven-a-side, never less than four-a-side. With the quality of players involved, the training was of a good standard. Greg Price and Will Antwi from the year above at Chace joined in. Will was kicking on at Crystal Palace while Tommy Morgan – newly signed at Orient –

was also involved. Vic's talented band of promising players naturally attracted the eyes of a number of professional clubs.

QPR were the first to get in contact with Vic about me. They invited me down to train with their centre of excellence and I jumped at the chance. After the longest year of my life, I couldn't wait to get back to proper football at a proper club. It was my chance to get going again. I was excited. There was a greater amount of caution there after the whole Chelsea fiasco, but the excitement far outweighed that caution.

I was moving on.

And so was Dad.

The posters accusing Terry remained stapled to the streets of Enfield but his energy was now being channelled into other ventures. There was his own soccer school, promising to teach pupils football in the Ajax way. He plastered himself on the flyers, wearing my Ajax top and Mizuno kit despite knowing nothing about football. He'd never taken a coaching badge and yet here he was trying to revolutionise youth football in the Enfield area.

Then there was his first record, promising to take the top 40 by storm. The thing was, Dad still had all of his contacts in the media. Over two years in the spotlight I'd appeared on pretty much every show and channel it was possible to. Now Dad was using that for his own benefit. First he appeared on *Kilroy*, talking about being the parent of a famous child. That was embarrassing. But it was nothing compared to his next move. Together with some mates he recorded a song that mainly featured him singing with his mates wolf whistling in the background. It was exactly the kind of tune which should never be taken seriously. So imagine my surprise when a classmate raced into Chase Community late one morning to announce that he'd just seen my dad on Channel 4's *Big Breakfast* promoting his new single. 'Leave it out, Dad,' I thought as I cringed into my school blazer. But at least he wasn't talking about me this time.

It was different going to football without Dad. When QPR found out that I'd struggle to get to training – Mum could only take me every now and again and the journey was a bit far for Terry – they invited another player from Vic's training sessions, Dan. A new ritual began, Dan's dad driving over to Willow Road to pick me up and take me over to training in west London. Those car journeys were long and the three of us spent the time chatting. Dan and his dad sat up in the front and I'd be on my own in the back. At first I enjoyed those chats, but as the weeks went by I became increasingly jealous. I'd listen to Dan and his dad chatting together and feel totally alone. They had their father-son relationship. The exact thing I used to love. The exact thing that had been taken away from me. It'd make me think back to all of those times me and Dad had gone to football together, our own little team ready to take over the world. In those moments I missed my father so much.

Without Dad, I was left to my own devices. I was free to do as I pleased. Yet even now the ban had finished and I was back chasing my dream at a proper professional club, the paranoia hadn't left. Those feelings that had crept in since the documentary couldn't be turned off and on like a switch.

Where's Dad?

I was constantly checking my shoulder to see if he was on the sidelines, a toxic mix of hope and fear.

They'll recognise me.

Being away from the spotlight meant that only a couple of my new team-mates instantly knew who I was. That was still enough for the pressure to ramp up.

I'm Sonny Pike the wonderkid. I need to play like it.

Football was no longer freedom. I could no longer just play with instinct. Instead, I was desperate not to mess up. The team at QPR was solid and I had to start off on the subs' bench. I had to force my way into the team by proving that I deserved a place. But in doing so I became more conservative. I knew my time was limited. Every week of the trial was another opportunity gone, another week closer to the inevitable decision. Fear of failure was growing and that resulted in heaps of nerves, which had never previously been an issue. Everything had seemed so easy before. It had only been a year but the game felt much faster. Everyone seemed to have grown much more than me in the same space of time. Could I really still be the wonderkid?

Not according to QPR. They stuck me out on the wing for the duration of my three-month trial. The coaches had seen all the footage from the cameras of me doing my skills and figured that was the obvious position for me. I didn't have the balls to tell them I was a striker.

We played against a lot of top teams and I did OK without ever really excelling. Still, I dared to dream. Maybe I could still get that contract, end up as a pro. I got my chance against Ipswich, playing from the start and scoring two goals. A game against West Ham, played at their training ground, really set me off. "Sonny, Sonny," people were shouting as we walked off at the end of the match, "Alex Ferguson's here!"

Jesus.

Fingers were being pointed and people were being nudged, all in the same direction. There was a bloke standing on the left-hand side of the pitch, the side I had been running up and down for the previous 45 minutes. It had only been just over a year since Alex Ferguson was in the audience as I collected my Sky Sports award. 'He must know who I am,' I thought. 'Maybe he's here to watch me?'

I had to find out if it really was him. While my team-mates all bounced back to the dressing room for their showers, still buzzing at the news, I made my way toward the figure.

With the game over, he'd moved on to the next pitch where a game was still going on. I got up close to him, too scared to say 'hello' but close enough that he'd see me there. That was all I wanted. Recognition. But he didn't turn. Instead, his eyes were locked on a player. It was Joe Cole. I followed Ferguson's eyes and then I followed Joe Cole. 'Fuck me,' I thought, 'he isn't half good.' He stood out like a sore thumb. You could just tell he was going to make it.

I went over to the pitch next to their match, closer to the Manchester United manager, and started kicking a ball around. Every now and again I'd look up. There was no doubt it was Alex Ferguson. But not once did he turn round. Not once did he do anything but watch Joe Cole. Soon I stopped kicking the ball around and followed Ferguson in watching. Joe Cole was magic, as if he could do what he wanted with the ball. Opponents were made to look silly. He was totally free, fearless, without a care in the world. Everything I used to be. Everything that I still wanted to be.

After that day I followed Joe's progress, and when I saw he was due to play against Leyton Orient I knew I had to be there. It felt like a million miles to get from Enfield to Leyton on public transport. I must have got at least three different buses. But I had to do it. I had to see Joe again. I had to size him up, see the competition, then learn from him.

While I was doing that, Alex Ferguson was sizing up a £10 million bid for him. For some reason it never materialised, but life didn't work out too badly for Joe.

At the end of my three months with QPR, no offer materialised. I never received a rejection from them but one of the coaches must have had a word with Dan's dad because once the three months were up we just stopped going.

Am I still a wonderkid?

Am I still any good?

Crystal Palace set up a satellite centre just down the road from me in Enfield, headed up by director of football John Cartwright. Terry got me to go along and, unlike at QPR, I did well from the very first session. Everything seemed to be set in place for me. I was in familiar surroundings, training alongside my mate from all of those years ago at Enfield, Adam 'Hitman'. He'd been bouncing around pro clubs such as Liverpool and Spurs since then, and after regularly playing against each other over the years we'd developed a mutual respect. On top of having some mates around, John also turned out to have an obsession with Ajax. He wanted his teams to get the ball down and play, just like Ajax. He'd show Adam videos of Edwin van der Sar playing the ball out from the back and ask Adam to replicate those techniques. Having the kid who played at Ajax, then, was a big coup for him. With each session the negative feelings that had plagued me started to disappear. The old feelings were returning. I was excelling. I was encouraged. I was the best player.

"Stop and look at what Sonny's doing," John used to say in training sessions. "That's how you do it. Try and copy him."

I grew 10 feet whenever he used to do that. Compliments became currency. Everything had calmed down. Football truly was my only focus.

I went with Palace to play Watford and had a blinder, so much so that Watford asked if I could play an age group above for them in their match that was about to kick off against Palace. The coaches didn't have a problem with it and soon enough I found myself lining up against my school-mate, Will Antwi, him in defence and me up front. Will was a decent defender, so much so that he ended up with a professional contract at Palace. Even so, I managed to score a headed goal in a 1-1 draw.

I was no longer excelling just in my age group.

More compliments came my way from the coaches at Palace. More nudges and pats on the back. More requests to "stop and watch Sonny".

The dream was back on.

I could still make it.

14: Swallowed Up

THE RUTHLESS FIGHT TO SIGN OUR SON BROKE MY HEART AND SMASHED THIS FAMILY APART

GEOFF SWEET REVEALS THE INDUCEMENTS TOP PREMIER LEAGUE CLUBS USE IN THEIR BID TO FIND SOCCER'S NEXT WONDERKID

THE NEWS OF THE WORLD, 17 JANUARY 1999

This is the harrowing story EVERY parent who dreams of turning their parent into soccer's next wonderkid HAS to read.

It is a story of broken promises, of relentless wheeler-dealing, pots of gold, secret inducements and, ultimately, the tragic disintegration of a once-happy family.

Of how that family were bombarded day and night with tantalising offers of jobs, flats, cars and holidays until, in the end, they no longer knew who to believe, who to trust – or who to turn to for advice. It's also the alarming story of how the country's biggest clubs will stop at nothing to transform the next wannabe into the next wonderkid.

As Joe Cole, 17, embarks on what everyone hopes will be a glittering career with West Ham and Jermaine Pennant, 15, gets his feet under the table at Highbury after his £2 million transfer from Notts County, ex-wonderkid Sonny Pike is facing a far from certain future.

His dad, Mickey, and mum, Stephanie, have split, and the dreams they shared of Sonny playing for a top club are as fragmented as their marriage.

"Football smashed up my family and broke my heart. What happened to us was terrible. It was like being on a runaway train heading for the buffers," said a tearful Mickey.

Two years. Two pages.

We stared at the double page spread in horror. Me, Mum and Terry. It had been such a long time since my name had been in the papers. We had all thought Dad had moved on. He hadn't. He'd been simmering, cooking away at this splash that would surely turn off professional clubs in their droves.

Ex-wonderkid.

I couldn't stop looking at that prefix. Ex. Was I already past my best at 15? That couldn't be right. Did they really think I'd never hit such heights again?

The article continued, Dad declaring that he was going to blow the whistle on the goings-on in the game so that other parents know what to expect before their sons kick a ball in professional football. At the top of the pages were photos of me and Mum, me with Prince Naseem, me with Ian Wright. But the biggest photo of all was of Dad, in action for his new soccer school, head to toe in branded gear and pointing at a football. The man never missed a trick.

"I could have been a rich man, with a new flat and car. They see someone with a bit of talent and offer anything.

"Forest offered me a job on the ground with a flat to get Sonny used to being up there.

"Many clubs were prepared to reimburse me up to £600 a week for losing work as a builder. Coventry were one of them. I told Blackburn about our holidays in a caravan in Yarmouth but was told: 'Go wherever you want – the Bahamas, no problem.'"

A warning sign was stamped on top of the article, urging anyone else to get in touch whose life had been ruined by a Premiership club trying to poach their wonderkid.

The warning sign didn't mention that my family had split up long before I'd ever kicked a ball.

It didn't say that I was desperate to play for a Premier League club, that I'd have done anything in my power to pull on the shirt of my beloved Liverpool, or Chelsea, or Manchester United, or anyone at the very top.

There was no suggestion that Dad – as I saw it – was the architect of my own downfall. Yet for the very clubs I dreamt of playing for, the conclusion from the article was obvious: this is a problem child with a problem family. Stay well away.

Mum was livid. Terry was seething. Dad was richer.

Family friends told that he was paid £23,000 for the article and used the money to buy a new Mercedes. We didn't know if it was true, but it didn't seem that unlikely to us.

"What a load of rubbish! They're picking on a kid. This has to stop now," Terry raged. "He's going to town. He's causing havoc. The Murdoch press is causing havoc. This has to be the final straw."

Mum nodded in agreement. No family should air their dirty laundry in the public eye. Something had to be done, no matter how drastic.

Like filing a lawsuit.

Mum took Dad to the Royal Courts of Justice over exploitation of their son. Try as she might, she was never going to keep that one away from the media.

MUM SUES DAD OVER KID SOCCER GENIUS: SHE WANTS HIIM BANNED FROM ACE, 15

EXCLUSIVE BY NEIL SYSON

THE SUN

A divorced couple are locked in a court battle over the future of their soccer genius son, tipped to become an all-time great.

Sonny Pike, 15, has been dubbed the next Alan Shearer and has League clubs, including FA Cup winners Chelsea, queuing to sign him.

But while builder dad Mickey, 45, has spent years promoting the youngster's football career, ex-wife Stephanie wants him to continue his studies at school.

Now Stephanie, 44, is to ask a judge at London's Royal Courts of Justice to ban Mickey from acting as Sonny's agent and mentor.

She said: "I thought Mickey was acting out of love – but then I realised he was chasing fame through his son.

"Sonny has a gift that needs nurturing, not exploiting, and I'll do what I must to protect him.

Sonny – seen juggling a football in McDonald's TV ads during Euro 96 – won a lucrative kit sponsorship deal at just 11. Dutch giants Ajax then invited him for a trial. And he earned an England youth World Cup place after bagging 340 goals in two seasons.

Dad Mickey says the youngster's football future could be wrecked if his mum wins the court ban in November.

But Stephanie, who lives with Sonny in Enfield, North London, said: "My son doesn't need an agent. He needs a bit of privacy to go to school and grow up.

"He was missing out on his childhood. If his talent is true, the fame and money will come later when he can cope."

Mickey no longer goes near Sonny, saying Stephanie has "brainwashed" his son against him.

He said: "Sonny has a unique talent and I've bent over backwards to do the best for him.

"I've sold the contents of my home to provide for his career. Now he's on the verge of turning professional.

"He needs total tunnel vision. But if my wife takes over, his whole career is in jeopardy."

Sonny said: "Dad furthered himself through me. He was living the life he wanted, thanks to my skills.

"I live for sport but he took the fun out of it."

The dirty laundry was getting dirtier. The public eye was getting larger.

Dad became desperate. One night he intercepted Terry on his dog walking route and handed him a note. 'If it's a magistrate say your worship, if it's a judge say your honour.' Terry screwed it up and threw it back at him.

"I can't go to the courts," my dad pleaded. "I'll have to be disguised."

"What the bloody hell! Who do you think I am?" Terry replied. "You're going to have to face the music at some point."

The court acted quickly. First, we were made to attend a family counselling session in Arnos Grove. Me, Mum and Dad all had to be in the same building at the same time and then go into the room with the counsellor separately. It was the first time I'd seen him in well over a year. In that small room I didn't know where to look: me and mum sitting on one side, Dad opposite us.

"Hello, son. How are ya?" he asked.

"All right, yeah," I mumbled in my most timid voice, not knowing where to look. The whole situation was so awkward. Dad hadn't changed at all. The power he held over all of us was still there to an extent. When I got called in to see the counsellor I felt so much relief. I wouldn't have to be in the same room as him.

"What do you want to do, Sonny?" the counsellor asked. She pretty much hinted that I had to choose between Mum and Dad. She was good, I'll give her that. There was something about her that I trusted, made me feel safe. Maybe it was her maternal nature, her quiet and gentle tone. Maybe it was her age, a friendly woman in her 50s that made me feel as if I was just talking to my nan.

I told her the whole situation was horrible. I hadn't asked for all of this. I just wanted to be a normal kid with a talent for football. A kid who played out with his mates and went home to his loving family while trying to achieve his dream of playing professional football.

I don't know what made me do it, but without realising what words were coming out of my mouth I was telling her all about that first trip to Holland and the time Dad hit me. I'd never told another living soul about that trip, not even Mum.

Fight or flight, and I'd chosen to fight.

Dad chose to fly.

The court case rambled on without him present. Terry gave evidence.

The judge ruled that Dad was no longer allowed to use my name in the media.

I could just concentrate on my football. Which, at the time, seemed the hardest thing to do. How can you possibly play with freedom while your family is in the middle of its own civil war?

It was too late. I laced up my golden Mizunos and attempted to kick on at Palace. But the Palace dream that had seemed so alive after the match against Watford soon crashed and burned. Just days after Dad's article I found myself desperate for the ground to swallow me up in a match against Spurs. Just weeks after Dad's article, with my service no longer required by Palace, I found myself barely able to leave my room. Just months after Dad's article I found myself cycling back from London with my friends. What had been a rare moment of happiness soon became darker as we approached Archway Bridge and I hung back from them.

The lure was strong. I dumped my bicycle and hauled myself up onto Suicide Bridge. The cars sped on below me. My feet remained planted to the cruel metalwork. The very same feet that had once had the world at them. The wind blew, strong enough to make me feel human. I held on tight and carried on looking below. Wondering whether to do it. The little voice urged me on.

Jump.

Jump.

What are you waiting for?

15: The Merry-Go-Round

Terry sat opposite me. Mum was on his left. Bucky on his right.

I didn't jump, but I knew I couldn't go much lower.

Yet in that lowest of lows, something had happened.

I'd finally grown some balls.

I'd finally admitted I needed help.

I was on the pathway to destruction, just like Dominique. Just weeks earlier she'd been sectioned under the Mental Health Act and placed into Chase Farm Hospital. From finding her own fame on Grange Hill, her life became increasingly chaotic as she became more involved with the wrong crowd, living the wrong kind of life. An adult at 15; sectioned at 20. Dad had lost his spy.

In recent months her behaviour had become even more unpredictable. She'd disappear for long periods, a law unto herself. Slowly, she became more aggressive to those who loved her the most. Paranoia increased. Somebody was going to get hurt. Enough was enough.

Our pathways were becoming more similar by the day.

I knew she was bad, but I only found out how bad when I went to visit her in the hospital with Bucky.

It terrified me. I didn't want to follow her through the front doors.

That's why I told Mum.

And that's why Mum got Terry and Bucky, my mate who'd been there since almost the first kick of my career.

They were sitting in my kitchen as I walked through the front door of the house, ball tucked under arm. The same kitchen that had been the focal point of the *Hello!* magazine shoot at the height of the media circus was now the setting for the lowest of my lows.

Terry was the first to speak. "Sonny," he said, "there's more to life than football. Don't worry about football. Enjoy your football." I looked around the room and saw three reassuring faces staring back at me. It was comforting. I felt safe in their presence. I knew they wanted the best for me. Their words were exactly what I needed to hear.

With them around me, the pressures that weighed me down so much faded momentarily: the football clubs treating me poorly because of a reputation earned by those around me, Dominique sectioned, Mum up and down, Mum's new boyfriend Joe on the scene, Dad disappearing, the money disappearing with him.

Mum and Bucky repeated Terry's sentiment and with every word I felt a weight lift from my shoulders. They were right. There was more to life than football.

"Whatever happens is going to happen," Mum advised.

"So don't worry about it. You don't need to race around everywhere at 100 miles-an-hour."

That was a trait I'd picked up from Dad. It meant I was prone to worrying. I agreed to take on a new mindset and enjoy life. I would no longer worry about football.

"There are other things you can do in this life," Terry added. "You could work as a chippy – a carpenter – or do the Knowledge and become a black cab driver. Go out with your mates. Do your own thing."

I don't know if his words were meant to be prophetic, but I ended up doing both of those jobs.

My new start began not with Terry, but with Bucky. In truth I'd been making it hard for Terry for a while – ever since Dad's article. I'd become erratic. He'd turn up to coach me and I'd be missing. In our sessions I'd train at half the pace I was capable of. Football had become a chore and Terry could see my head was gone. Bucky was a chance to start fresh. He'd been getting into his coaching and had given me a few sessions since leaving Loughton. No matter how many sessions we'd have though, Bucky would always be my mate first and my coach second. Recognising that, Terry advised me to go off and enjoy myself. He understood my need for change. And it wasn't like he was going out of my life. He still came round the house regularly to say hello to me and Mum and walk the dog. We began to play golf together. Terry was a member down the local club and gave me gentle advice but I didn't have the patience to be much good. Still, we enjoyed our times on the course and did our best to not talk about football. Terry even began to come round the house on Christmas Day, a new tradition to add to the already established tradition of Bucky coming round as well.

Our set-up was mutually beneficial. Bucky had first got into coaching when he was working as a lifeguard at a leisure centre in Pickett's Lock, Enfield. Eager to make a bit of extra cash, he got chatting to one of the coaches who rented the artificial pitch and specialised in Coerver coaching. Coerver coaching, Bucky discovered, is a method created by 1970s Dutch coach Wiel Coerver that involves developing individual skills and team play through ball manipulation. Most importantly, however, he discovered that the coach needed a bit of help with a few sessions.

Bucky jumped at the chance and soon he caught the bug. He continued to coach and play at college, but a bad leg break left him in plaster cast for eight months. Rather than mope about, Bucky spent those eight months taking advantage of a new innovation: dial-up internet. Patiently waiting for the phone line to become free, he searched the internet for stories of how top footballers he admired became so skilful. He watched videos to see how David Beckham, Dennis Bergkamp and Zinedine Zidane moved, how they touched the ball, how they did things. He read on as Bergkamp told how he trained obsessively against a wall to perfect his control and skill. He soaked it all up and then wrote to 50 professional clubs asking for a chance. His decision had been made. He knew he was never going to become a decent football player but thought he could have opportunities in coaching. Barnet and Luton both got back to Bucky's letter and asked him to come down so they could take a look. As soon as he was out of plaster he went up to Luton but found the journey a bit far. Barnet, however, was much more like it. The centre of excellence director Gary Karsa snapped Bucky right up and soon enough he was coaching seven days a week in both their football in the community scheme and centre of excellence.

Against that backdrop, we started our one-on-one sessions at Furzefield Leisure Centre in Potters Bar, where Bucky worked in his full-time job. Bucky was helping me to get back to where I wanted to be while I was helping Bucky to become a better coach at the beginning of his career. The timing was perfect as our worlds aligned. In many ways, I was his guinea pig. All of the information he'd absorbed while in plaster cast he implemented and trialled on me. We had access to the entire leisure centre and he'd have me whipping balls on the artificial pitch, then rebounding passes and executing turns in the squash court to replicate Bergkamp's training.

At the same time, Bucky was repeating his letter writing trick.

He wrote to a whole range of professional clubs asking them to take a chance on Sonny Pike. Cambridge were the first to respond, their head of youth Ricky Martin inviting me up for three weeks. When it soon emerged he didn't fancy me, Bucky pulled me out and took me over to Wycombe. Over the next few months we must have done about 7,000 laps of the M25 in Bucky's crusty old Astra. It took bloody ages to get to Bisham Abbey where Wycombe trained, a right schlep from Enfield. Even so, we loved it. For both of us, the hunt for a contract proved to be a really enjoyable time. We were two mates preparing to drive anywhere for a slice of the dream. The car journeys were a laugh, a chance to relax and have some quality conversations. That in itself was important. Even though our whole purpose was football, we never spoke about football in that car.

Bucky organised everything but he never told me I had to do anything. I was free to make my own decisions and that freedom was important. For the first time, I wasn't around grown-ups who were making all of my decisions for me. And Bucky, just like Terry, had my best interests at heart. "You're my pal, I'd do anything to help you," he'd often say.

Two weeks into our long drives to Bisham Abbey, we found out that Wycombe were interested in giving me a YTS.

As a centre-back.

They wanted to trial me out in defence. I'd never heard a crazier suggestion but I went along with it. They stuck me at centre-back for their next match and I did my best to give the Wycombe coach a heart attack. I was Cruyff turning in my own penalty area and dribbling out from defence to try and beat about 46 opponents.

"You were just like Matthias Sammer!" Bucky laughed in the car. We both knew my Wycombe experience was over. They were a long ball team and wanted their centre-backs to hit the channels. I wanted to do anything but. Especially not if I had to play in defence. There's nothing enjoyable about preventing goals rather than scoring them.

Next up on our tour was Brentford. That one was a bit awkward for Bucky because the coach in charge was the same coach whose job Bucky had taken at Barnet. Not that it mattered because Brentford turned out to be an absolute shambles. The journey was horrendous, the standard not great. We got out pretty sharpish.

Barnet followed, which was a natural fit thanks to Bucky. He was coaching the U12s and U14s over there while Paul Davis was the U16 manager. Paul was actually employed by Arsenal but worked with the younger age groups over there. Barnet allowed him to coach an older age group so that he could pass his UEFA A Licence coaching badge.

Bucky desperately wanted me to succeed with Paul and Barnet. I knew he thought it'd be a waste if I packed in football. "Just go down and see what you think of it. Remember, you just have to enjoy it. There's no pressure," he'd always tell me when a new opportunity came up. Mainly, though, Bucky was driven by the voices he heard on the other side of the astroturf. While I was on the pitch, Bucky heard everything the parents said. "He's a problem." "What's he doing here?" "He won't last here." To Bucky's credit, he never told me about all of the judgmental opinions he heard. They made him so angry. They were judging me on my history and making me deal with the consequences of others' actions. So were the clubs. Bucky believed that I'd been the best player at every single club I'd trialled with. But when I walked through the front door, my reputation walked in with me. The words of Dad's *News of the World* article still rang loud. Problem boy. Warning sign. Avoid.

Nobody knew the full story. Worse still, they didn't want to know the full story. When they saw me play football they didn't see Sonny the player, they saw Sonny the personality.

They didn't need to see anything else.

But Barnet could be different. With the Bucky link, we both felt the focus would be on Sonny the player.

Safe in that knowledge, I slotted right in. Within five games I was top scorer and I could tell the others were impressed. Any pressure that had been put on me by those expecting to see Sonny the personality was well and truly lifted.

The day arrived when the club would announce those they'd chosen to take on scholarship forms. We gathered at Bucky's workplace, Furzefield Leisure Centre, that doubled up as Barnet's training ground. Players waited in the bar area with their mums and dads but mainly their dads as they waited to be called into the office one by one. Nobody came with me. I was alone. I watched on as my team-mates went in one by one, each of them entering hopefully and leaving devastated. No. No. No. No. So many dreams crushed in such little time. "Waste of time," the latest to be rejected told me. "I've not got it. I'm telling you right now that nobody has got one apart from the gaffer's son."

I never even walked in for my meeting after that. The gaffer's son wasn't only the first-team gaffer's son, but also the other striker in the team. The same one that I'd only needed five games to outscore for the whole season.

Not to worry. I'd take it on the chin.

The football merry-go-round was in full swing. In clubs

up and down the country, promising young players were being rejected for YTS forms. Refusing to be beaten, those players began their own tours around professional clubs in the hopes of achieving their dream elsewhere, just like me and Bucky had been doing for the best part of six months.

Still, Bucky had another trick up his sleeve: a trial at non-league Stevenage. They were holding an exit trial that June to identify promising players released by professional clubs. Those successful would take on a two-year YTS which involved studying on a college course at Hitchin while training full-time with Stevenage's youth team.

As often happened, I turned up to the trial at Stevenage's training ground in Letchworth late. My mates often joked that I'd arrive late to my own funeral. I probably would, to be fair. Up at Letchworth it was more or less a case of heading straight out onto the pitch. From my first touch I just knew. It's often the way with football. It's a game of instinct. Some days everything just feels right: the pitch, the conditions, the feel of the ball. I played with freedom, buoyed by the news that Dominique had been released from hospital. Her plight had put everything into perspective. Football had to be fun. I couldn't feel pressure to perform. Enjoyment should be everything. If it wasn't, and I remained on the path I had previously been on, there was every chance I'd end up following in her footsteps. And so I ran around the pitch with a smile. I lollipopped and Cruyff turned and scissored my way through the defence. Players actively looked for me to pass to. Get the ball. Where's Sonny? Find him. On the sidelines, former Wales and Newcastle striker Malcolm Allen watched on. He was contracted to Stevenage's first team and had obviously been roped in to advise the club on certain aspects.

"Son," he told me as I walked off the pitch. "There's more talent in your little toe than I've seen in anyone else who's put on the Stevenage shirt."

That was enough to encourage me that Stevenage was the right place.

And I'd more than encouraged Stevenage that I was the right player.

Bucky was thrilled. He praised Stevenage for taking all context out of their decision, for judging it on Sonny the player rather than Sonny the personality. I was pretty chuffed too. The two-year course that I enrolled in ended up being exactly what I needed. My new team-mates were a great bunch, always laughing and joking with each other. Most of them were from up in Hertfordshire, but to my delight Adam 'Hitman', my former team-mate from Palace and Enfield Colts, had also been offered a YTS. After his release he'd embarked on his own journey to win a scholarship at a professional club. From a positive start, the rejections soon mounted up and left him wondering whether he actually wanted to play football, whether he really was any good. Like me, Stevenage had been his last chance of success. And like me, he'd taken it.

With me safely up and running at Stevenage, Bucky left me a bit more to my own devices when it came to football. He'd been offered a role at Arsenal with the U9s that took up more of his time. When we did get together we did so socially. He'd tell me all about the new players he was coaching: Benik Afobe, Ryan Fredericks, Harry Kane. Then he'd ask about Stevenage, whether I was getting on all right.

Mum's boyfriend Joe had moved in with us by this point and he'd look after me, giving me a bit of pocket money each day so I could catch the train from Chase Side to Hitchin via Stevenage with Adam. Adam would get the bus over to mine and then we'd have a little mooch, slow it right down if we were due to be in college, speed it right up if we were meant to be training that morning. The more we did that journey, the closer we became until eventually we were living in each other's pockets. At first we formed a tight group with the two other lads from round London, Jake Panayiotous and Lee Dignan, or Diggers, as we called him. Everyone else was from around Hertfordshire and settled into their own cliques. As me and Adam had both been at professional clubs we were seen as the big timers. They didn't realise that our past had disadvantaged us. The rejections we'd suffered had left us scarred, wondering if we were still good at football, no longer desperate to put ourselves in a position where we could be hurt again. Not like them, good local players with a point to prove and dreams still unbroken. We might have had the superior technical ability, but they had far more of the bollock and bite that is valued in the lower leagues. All we could do in that scenario was get our heads down and show our true character. Once we'd proved ourselves to them, proved that we weren't big time and were after the same thing as them, they opened up until we became one big unit.

With those new relationships, the football side of things became secondary. Which was just as well because, when I joined up with Stevenage, Malcolm Allen had left the club and then, in my first month of playing, I suffered my first-ever injury. It was a pre-season friendly against Millwall and I went to put the ball down the line, only for my hamstring to explode. It felt like someone had shot me. There was no chance of carrying on, and I was confined to the physio's table for a good few weeks.

I no longer felt devastated at being unable to play football. Everything seemed more relaxed. Having new mates around me and a more settled home life did wonders for my mental state. The paranoia disappeared. I felt happier than I had for years.

When I returned from injury I put myself about a bit in games but the burning desire was no longer there. The coaching staff liked me and Adam in particular. They put us in to train with the first team and called us up to play in the FA Youth Cup, making us some of the only first years to ever play in the cup for the club. And we almost didn't make it. Adam had the bright idea to drive us to the game in his dad's motor even though he hadn't passed his test. He arrived at mine in sheer panic, refusing to turn the engine off. "I don't know what to do!" he yelled. "I can't drive it!" Between us we'd had about four lessons but, seeing as Adam was so shaken up, we decided I'd drive the car back to his house and then let Adam's dad take us to the game. Like Adam, I didn't know what I was doing either and so I drove back to his house with the clutch down the whole way. The engine completely flooded, so much so that when Adam's dad did come back from work the car wouldn't start. "What's gone on here then?" he asked. We just shrugged. "Dunno."

A few frantic phone calls later and Adam's dad had sourced a car to take us over to Colchester for the match. Playing in the FA Youth Cup provided a welcome chance to test myself, but once that was gone I settled into a habit of playing for fun. Perhaps our team-mates had been right to see me and Adam as big timers. Having seen the comparative luxuries at other clubs we developed the mindset that Stevenage was a bit Mickey Mouse. As a result, we didn't make the best of the situation, preferring to have a laugh rather than striving to make it. At least we had some great times along the way. Our coaches were brilliant and gave us some wicked experiences, including taking the whole team abroad to Spain to compete in a tournament. Rooming with Adam, we noticed that our midfielder Eddie, whose room was next door, always left his window wide open.

"We've got to do something about that," Adam said.

On an afternoon when we knew Eddie was out, we climbed together across the roof, scaling the building and risking certain death before dropping safely through the window and into the room. That was when the laughs really began. Eddie always wore half a tub of gel in his hair, spiking it up so it always looked as if he'd just received an electric shock. Sniggering, we located Eddie's hair gel tub, unscrewed it, and proceeded to ejaculate into it. The deed done, we mixed it in with the hair gel before screwing the top back on and returning to our room.

The next day we were in stitches when Eddie came down to breakfast with his hair spiked up as usual. We didn't stop laughing the whole way to the game, nor for the whole first half. It was only in the second half that Adam mentioned what had happened.

That was the kind of thing that happened all the time.

That was normal at Stevenage, and as the months went by my life felt more and more normal.

Glimpses of hope still appeared. Our coaches at Stevenage promised me and Adam that they wouldn't stand in the way if a bigger club came along. I had some sniffing around, then Adam received a concrete offer from Bristol Rovers. They invited him to play a game, liked what they saw but then the situation hit a brick wall. Stevenage said they wanted money for Adam. That was never going to happen. Bristol Rovers weren't much better off than Stevenage, certainly not flush enough to be spending money on teenage goalkeepers. The deal was off, and Adam's head was off with it. He was stuck.

The first year melted away and we became second years, the leaders. It was on us to set the standards. Adam was particularly frustrated by a new first year who wore a massive bracelet into the changing rooms and even trained with it on. We both agreed that it was unprofessional, yet when we told him so he wasn't having any of it. Adam waited patiently, then when the first year was in the shower he grabbed the lad's pot of moisturiser and took a dump in it. Then we played the waiting game. The player emerged from the shower, towelled off and reached for his wash bag. He opened the moisturising pot, looked inside, then screwed it back up and acted like nothing had happened. He never did say anything about it, but it was the last time any of us ever saw the bracelet.

Was it 'banter'? Yes. Was it right? Probably not. But that was football back then, 'character building'.

As more of the group turned 18, we sampled more of the north London nightlife. I was still largely teetotal, focused on my football enough to continue living a healthy lifestyle. On those nights out I had the occasional drink but never really got drunk. The same couldn't be said of Adam. We had some great nights together and my house on Willow Road soon became our base. I was mad on my music by that point. Garage, house and rap especially. Having dabbled in rapping all those years ago, I now had decks up in the loft. We'd be pumping out music, Joe would be making us up cocktail mixes in a big bowl and then we'd head out into the night with a bit of spending money from Joe. The next morning, Joe delighted in hearing the stories while grilling up the bacon, whereas Mum would stroke Adam's hair and tell him it was all going to be okay. With groups of young lads learning their limits there were often entertaining stories. There were also plenty of stories of violence too. The sixth sense that I'd developed all those years ago came into its own. If we were out in Enfield it tended to be okay. People knew me. A little further afield, in places such as Essex or Watford, people recognised me but didn't know me. They thought I was still a footballer, a big-time Charlie living the high life, and wanted to bring me down a peg. We had a lot of punch-ups. My sixth sense became even more acute and I found that I could sense when the atmosphere changed in a room. A group of lads eyeing me up in the corner. Someone approaching me, breathing down my neck. Fortunately, we often had strength in numbers. And if the worst happened, we'd always meet back at my house in Willow Road. There was a bit of an open-door policy. I even gave some of my team-mates keys to the house. If ever we were split up on a night out, the rule was to always meet back at mine – even if I wasn't there. One night that backfired on Martin, our central-midfielder from Stevenage, when he tried to get through the front door long after we were all home. Joe thought the house was being robbed and confronted the poor lad with a machete.

When you're onto a good thing, it can only last for so long. Towards the end of my two years, we were all called into the first-team ground where we would be told our fate. Excitement was in the air, but mainly there was caution. For many this was the end of what had been an incredible two years. And for some it was only going to be the beginning.

That's what we thought, anyway. An hour later the mood had totally transformed. Not one person was offered a contract with the first team. A few of us were invited back for pre-season in the hope of winning a non-contract with the team, but that felt like a cop-out. None of us were going to be footballers. My team-mates were all gutted, proper upset. And yet I felt like a weight had been lifted from my shoulders. I didn't have to be a footballer. No, not even that. I couldn't be a footballer. I didn't have to play football anymore. I could leave the sport for good. I'd given it a go and hadn't been good enough. I'd burned myself out with all that had come before Stevenage, which had made me spend more of the two years enjoying myself. I'd had fun, and now it was over. Instead of sharing in my team-mates' disappointment, I found myself consoling them.

I could be normal.

16: Acting Up

I could leave the sport for good. But it was easier said than done. Pro Tech got in contact with me. It was a college course and full-time training programme for footballers. I wasn't really interested until I found out I could just train and not do the college course. Then when I was told their coach, Alex Inglethorpe, could sort me with a few games for Barnet at the end of the season I took them up on the offer. To their credit, they were true to their word.

I signed a contract with Barnet – the first I'd ever signed by myself – to play in the final eight games of the season. The first team had been relegated to the Conference the season before but I'd mainly be with the reserves. In my first match they put me straight into the thick of it at centre midfield. We were playing against Crystal Palace's reserves and I had a tough opponent that day in Wayne Routledge. Still, I did well in my unfamiliar position. The pitch at Underhill really suited me. Mainly because it was small so I didn't have to run about very much, but also because its compactness created a more technical, passing game. At the same time I turned out for Pro Tech, and in one of my matches for them a watching scout from Birmingham City took interest. So much so that he turned up at my house after the match, just like in the old days when the scouts would flock to my front door. He introduced himself and said he'd love to get me up to the Midlands. Things were happening. But just as quickly they weren't. The season finished and interest petered out from Barnet and Birmingham. I heard rumours that Pro Tech had demanded money from Birmingham but never discovered the truth.

As far as I was concerned, that was the end of football. I started labouring. It was tough work, long days, but I found camaraderie on site. It was a laugh, just like my previous two years at Stevenage. I settled down and vowed to do the best job I possibly could.

Summer was closing out when I received a phone call from an unknown number. I answered it to find that Sky Andrew, the Olympian turned agent who engineered Sol Campbell's controversial move from Tottenham to Arsenal and also brought hot young talent Jermaine Pennant to the Gunners, was on the line.

"Hello Sonny," he said. "I've got something for you. Why don't you come down to my office in Woodford?"

There was nothing to lose. I shrugged my shoulders and arranged a time and date. I might as well see what he had to say. If I liked it then I was free to do as I pleased. If I didn't then I wasn't bound by anything. There'd be nobody else in my ear making me do something I didn't want to do. It would be my own decision.

Best of all, the trip meant I got to have a little runout in my brand-new car, a nice little Golf with a v5 engine that

I hadn't had long. Try as I might, I couldn't really see a downside.

I arrived in Woodford still buzzing about my new car. But as soon as I stepped out of the driver's seat the apprehension began to build. That apprehension only grew further when I was shown into Sky's office.

"I thought you was black," Sky exclaimed when he locked eyes on me. I looked myself up and down. Did he actually mean to say that or was he thinking out loud?

"Sorry, mate."

What else could I say? I walked up to his desk and shook his hand, then offered my hand to the young Greek man on Sky's right-hand side, who introduced himself as Cos Phillips. Sky took my hand and then regained his composure as I sat down.

"What are you doing then? Where do you reckon you can play, what sort of standard? Because I'm going to be honest with you, if you can't play in the Premier League or Division One then I can't do anything for you." Sky obviously wasn't one for slow introductions. I knew his type. I'd come across so many agents and knew the words they wanted to hear.

"Well I think I can play at the top. Technically I'm good enough and if I'm fit enough I can play anywhere I want."

Sky nodded without taking in what I'd said. I had to focus on the positives, not on all of my struggles and problems. But he seemed to have lost interest before I'd even finished my sentence.

"Okay. Well Cos wants to speak to you," he nodded at the man next to him. "I'll leave you two to it."

Sky didn't get up. Instead Cos ushered me into another meeting room. Straight away, he had me interested. He told me about this show called *Dream Team*. It was on Sky One and had been hugely successful, though he didn't have to point that out. Of course I'd heard of the fictional Premier League side that played in purple, Harchester United. I'd even seen some of the episodes. And now Cos wanted me to make an appearance on Dream Team. Playing myself.

All right.

The following week was red hot. Scorching. Summer had made its final, vicious comeback before the long days became long nights. I drove to Woodford, where I was set to meet Cos at the office. He'd then drive me in his new Mercedes Jeep to an audition to play myself. It felt surreal. It felt exciting. For once, I was doing something on my own terms. We hadn't even discussed money. I didn't have a clue if I was getting paid for the audition. All I knew was it sounded interesting and that's all that mattered. It wasn't like I was going to be nervous in front of the cameras. I doubted anyone had had more training with them than me.

For some reason, I hadn't expected them to ask me to play football in my audition. I thought I'd turn up, pretend to be myself for a bit and then either get the part or be rejected. But the first thing they did was chuck me a ball and ask me to do some skills. I couldn't have come less prepared. If anything it had got even hotter and I was wearing totally the wrong clothes. My grey Mickey Mouse jumper and blue jeans weren't the most heat resistant, and as I attempted to juggle the flat pancake that masqueraded as a ball I worked up quite a sweat. Grey, it turned out, was not the ideal colour. Still, they asked me to carry on, sweat patches and all. More skills, more dribbling, how about some free-kicks? My grey jumper was sopping wet by the time I was told to call it a day with the ball. Then I was ushered inside to recite some lines.

It soon became obvious that out of the two, football was my forte. I tried my hardest at the reading but the words occasionally jumbled together. It felt far from natural. The director had a word with Cos, who then relayed what he said once we were safely back in his car on the way to Woodford. The director liked me and thought my character could have a greater role in the show. My acting, though, needed to improve. That was fine. Everyone needs practice. Cos would recommend an acting class for me to join. I'd cut my teeth there and then return to Dream Team when I was ready. There could be a future there for me if I was willing to work for it.

A week later I found myself 15 minutes down the road from my mum's house at Bodens Performing Arts College in Barnet, named after the actor Tony Boden. The same drama school that Dominique attended all those years ago. What did I have to lose? In part, I still wanted to make something of myself. Much of it, though, was the desire to keep myself away from a life I knew it was only too easy to fall into. Drink, drugs, pubs and clubs, temptation had already suckered in many of my mates. I'd joined them occasionally in the pubs for a laugh and a drink but that's where I drew my line. I didn't want to go any further.

The drama school was based in this little hall with a proper stage at the front. A circle was formed of 15 people sitting on old wooden chairs, and as I introduced myself they welcomed me in. As the session went on I got to hear the stories of those around me. Many had been coming for years. Acting was their passion. As for me? I was a complete fish out of water. Though I'd had all my experience in front of cameras and also visited Dominique, not long out of the psychiatric unit, to ask for advice from her *Grange Hill* days, I was still far behind everyone else. They had me reading out lines from Shakespeare, which was hard enough without half of the words being in a foreign language. I didn't know what most of them meant! Improv was more my thing. We were split into small groups then set a scene for us to act out as we pleased. I got right into that, so much so that I was a little disappointed when the session ended. I was already looking forward to the following week. So long as there wasn't any Shakespeare involved.

Back on site I told the other labourers about drama school. They were asking all questions and showing interest. 'Deadly' Dave Owens mentioned Grimsby again. It must have been the 10th time he'd said it. He had a mate up there who was involved in the football club and could get me a trial. I'd always politely turned him down before, but now that everything was looking up I thought, 'Why not?' After all, it was a good chance to take my new Golf on a nice long road trip.

"Go on then, Deadly," I said. "I'll go to Grimsby."

"I'll sort it," he replied.

Deadly was as good as his word. The following week I was due up to Grimsby for training on the Monday morning. I wanted this to be different, though. I'd been chewed up and spat out of football so many times that something needed to change. And so on the Sunday evening I got out a pair of clippers and set them to 0.5. If I was returning to football, I wouldn't be doing so as Sonny Pike.

The long curls fell to the floor. By the time I was done there was barely anything up top. I was a skinhead, unrecognisable from that curly haired kid who ended up being a media darling. That one who was supposed to be better than Best.

Sonny was gone.

He'd been replaced by Luke.

I left early the next morning, before the birds had even had a chance to start singing from the trees. By 6.30am I was in Grimsby. Deadly's contact at the club had sorted me out with some accommodation for the week. I parked up and managed to find the key for this little house I was to be put in. I waited for daylight to break, then took a walk along the beach beside the house. It was different up there, that much was for certain. I didn't often go so far north. The reality began to hit me. What the hell was I doing in Grimsby?

I was scheduled to meet my new team-mates at 9.30am in the changing rooms at the stadium. My first-ever taste of professional football as Luke. To pass the time I strolled up and down the beach, the cold breeze from the Humber startling me.

"Sonny, how are you?" the coach asked as soon as I walked into the changing room. "Have a seat."

Fuck.

My cover had been blown already.

"That's my nickname," I replied. "Call me Luke."

"I don't know what he's on about," I told the geezer I sat next to. "My name is Luke."

"All right, Luke?" he asked before getting back to kitting up.

That message soon spread. The skinhead in the corner wanted to be called Luke, not Sonny. The coaches heard it too. They called me by my new name as we went back to the beach I'd walked on earlier that morning for a series of physical exercises. My team-mates grimly went about the tasks. A mix of youths and reserve team players, they knew they had to put the work in, no matter how unappealing it was. Anything to impress.

The afternoon was much more like it. Training was conducted on the first-team pitch and consisted of passing drills and a bit of a kickabout. I fitted in fine. This was easily my level. I was comfortable.

With the day's training over, there was nothing to do but return to my little temporary house and wait for the morning to come. It was so boring, just waiting for time to pass. Dinner wasn't provided and so I went to the chippy down the road. That was eye-opening. The people in the chippy were battering anything they wanted. I'd never seen anything like it. Customers were coming in and asking for deep-fried Mars bars. And the people behind the counter weren't batting an eyelid. What the hell was going on? These people were nuts. That's all I could think. Where have I come to? What are these people like?

Maybe it was an immaturity thing but I was freaked out before seeing that, let alone after. That night I tossed and turned, the same thought bouncing around my head. What am I doing here? What is this place? I don't belong here.

At 3am I couldn't take it anymore. I still hadn't slept a wink. What was the point? Even if I was successful with my trial, I couldn't stay in a place like this. Not somewhere so alien. And even if I could, I'd never be able to change my identity. I'd never be Luke. Only Sonny. I got up, picked up my bags, walked straight out of the door and never went back. I got into my Golf and drove away from Grimsby forever. Away from football forever.

17: Born Slippy

My life settled into the same routine. Labouring during the week, drama school on Friday evenings and a bit of wheeler-dealing with the odd pub and club visit mixed in at the weekend. If my mates had it any other way, I'd have been spending much more of my time with them in the pubs and nightclubs around north London. It was tempting. With football gone, the acting was the only thing holding me back.

The first six weeks at Tony's school were turning into a slog. My improv had gone from strength to strength but I was still stumbling over Shakespeare. No matter what happened, each week there'd always be something old-fashioned in the lesson. Having to stand up and say all these words that were no longer words seemed pointless. I was hardly going to need to recite a poem from 300 years ago on *Dream Team*, was I?

Attending the session each week was becoming hard. I had to really push myself to keep going. Unlike those around me. Excitement was growing in the class with the announcement that we were to put on our own play. Tickets would be sold locally and there'd be a bit of press on the night. Everyone was given the option of taking part and everyone agreed they would like to take part, myself included. Roles were assigned and we started our rehearsals for the big show.

'Just keep doing it,' I repeated over and over. 'You can still make something of yourself. Give the show a go. You might like it.'

Then the Shakespeare lines came out and it proved to be the final straw. All of the pep talks I'd given myself went out the window. What was I doing in this old hall, trying to act? Who did I think I was? I was done. Finished.

I knew where my mates were. It was Friday night. They'd been going on about it all week.

The teacher paused the class so we could all take a quick break. I excused myself, stood up, walked out of the door and never went back. I got in my Golf and rang my mates up.

"Where are you?" I asked, though I already knew. They'd be at the George in Enfield. "Listen, I'm coming to meet you." I could hear the cheers in the background.

My head was all over the place.

I'd tried football and nothing had happened.

I'd tried acting and nothing had happened.

Nothing was ever going to happen. There was only one thing I could do, only one thing I wanted to do: let loose and feel free.

For the first time in my life, I removed all limitations. I'd never been drunk before, but soon enough I was knocking them back with my mates. We had a few drinks in The

George before heading over to a nightclub in Gants Hill called Faces. That was enough to get me going. I was putting away the pints just like all my mates around me. The beer was horrible, like gone-off fizzy water and so I changed to vodka and Red Bull. That was better. Just like the drinks, soon enough the world seemed a better place. Everything was better. My seal broken, I went for a piss and a random man next to me tapped my shoulder and held out a credit card. There was a little corner of white powder on it.

Straight away, I knew what it was.

I'd seen drugs before but never touched them. Some of my mates had started dabbling and they were always knocking around the pub scene. There'd be scores upon scores of scrunched up lottery tickets lining the floor of The George's toilets. At first I thought it was because the drinkers there loved playing the lottery, but over time I realised it was because their drugs came wrapped in tickets.

That was all different. The drugs were around me but never in front of me. I stared at the white powder sitting there inches in front of my nose. For about a second. Before I knew it, the white powder had gone and a mad rush of energy had built up inside me. It was just what I'd wanted. To feel free. To be just like my mates. As the geezer made his way out of the toilets and I followed him there was no regret. I was past caring. For the first time in my life the gloves were well and truly off.

When I got back to my mates they were all at the bar speaking to another group of lads. "Oi, there's this illegal rave going on at Trent Park," I could hear them saying. "Do you boys fancy it?" My mates were all nodding their heads and I was in agreement. It sounded exciting.

We left the club and hailed a set of taxis to take us to the country house of Trent Park, just east of Enfield. Within its 413 acres of rolling country parkland was our ultimate destination. The rave.

Ten of us were dropped in the middle of a field in Trent Park. We were all dressed up to the nines, ready for a big night out in our best jeans, belts, collared shirts and fancy shoes. Exactly the kind of get-up you don't want to be traipsing over muddy fields in. We squelched our way into the forest, sometimes stepping in puddles, often getting stuck in the mud. Our jeans were getting covered.

Then we heard it. Thud. What was that? We all stopped, desperately listening out for confirmation of what we heard. Thud. There it was again. Thud. Thud. Thud.

We went mad. There it was. The rave! We could hear it. We had to follow the music.

It was pitch-black in that forest. The trees were tall, the bushes thick. Still we ploughed on, determined to find the source of the sound.

The thud gave way for a boom. Boom! Boom! Boom! And then we were out of the forest and into a clearing and there it was, the rave. People were everywhere. Proper 'out there' people, the kind with spiked hair dyed purple and piercings all over the place. They were wearing all the colours of the rainbow and as they blurred together in movement the music took over. It was no longer a thud or a boom. It was a song, the lead song from *Trainspotting*, played from the makeshift DJ decks and amplified by the speakers all around.

Let your feelings slip boy
But never your mask boy
Random blonde bio high density rhythm
Blonde boy blonde country blonde high density
You are my drug boy
You're real boy
Speak to me and boy dog
Dirty numb cracking boy

The lyrics from Underworld's *Born Slippy* echoed around my head. I'd stopped in my tracks. My mates were all entranced. This was what we'd been searching for. It was better than what we could ever have imagined. Letting loose was better than I ever could have imagined. Why had I been so uptight and focused on my football all of that time? Why hadn't I been out with my mates doing this?

The trees moved in time to the music. Above us a sprawl of army netting rustled in the wind, the makeshift leaves attached to it adding to the incredible sensation of my surroundings. Bed sheets hung all around us to create the impression of a wall, paint flicked up everywhere. Lager, lager, lager. We'd joined together and were jumping around. My mate Ben Collins couldn't get over the bed sheets. He was poking them, convinced they were walls. Then he leant against the sheet and went toppling over. Lager, lager, lager. Everything about the place was mental.

The rainbow-coloured ravers welcomed us into their sanctuary. They passed us laughing gas and pills with a Mitsubishi sign and we thanked them and inhaled and ingested. I felt a pure sense of living in the moment. I turned down the laughing gas but didn't think twice before swallowing half a pill, then when it had no effect I didn't think twice before swallowing the other half. That was better. Within 20 minutes an amazing sensation had spread throughout my body. I was coming up. I no longer knew what song was playing. *Born Slippy* was still bouncing around my head. Mega, mega white thing. I didn't want to stand up. I laid down on the mud and cuddled up to my mates. My whole body was sighing in happiness, as if I was melting into a warm bath in the middle of the cold forest. They were all in a state of bliss, either curled up into balls or talking with sheer joy to one another.

I wanted to lay there forever. I never wanted the feeling to end.

But end it had to. As the darkness turned to light the rave wound down. The music slowed to a boom, then a thud, then silence. Ravers made their way out of the forest. There was nothing for us to do but follow them all the way to the bus stop.

"Thanks so much for having us," we told them.

"Not at all, we loved having you," they replied.

It was incredible. All these hippies, ravers and rockers with purple hair and piercings that I'd never normally interact with talking to us and having a laugh. We spoke the whole way home, laughing on the upper deck of the bus and vowing to do it all again.

The following day I met up with my mates in The George and we agreed to go in search of the rave once more. There was no regret on my behalf. I'd felt what it was to be normal and I wanted to chase that feeling over and over again.

We spent the next three weeks trying to recreate our night, even returning to the same field in Trent Park. There was nobody there. The rave had gone. Our friends had disappeared. We were chasing something that wasn't there.

18: Real Football

Pre-season came and went. For the first time I let it pass me by. I didn't even kick a ball in anger. Why should I? I didn't miss it. Football was my past. It was time to find my future.

I barely even knew what was happening in football. Gone were the days when I obsessively ate up anything to do with the sport.

I no longer watched games. Sometimes I'd flick through the sport pages and see how Joe Cole, Scott Parker, David Bentley or any of the people I'd once been compared to were getting on. I'd read the headlines about the growing number of foreign imports and the harder path to the top for talented Brits. I'd hear about the fall of ITV Digital and the terrible impact it had on clubs like Leyton Orient. Mentions of a Russian man called Roman Abramovich being interested in Chelsea filtered through. But it all went in one ear and out the other. Football was just a thing.

I was happy with my life. In the pub with all the fellas at lunchtime and after work, walking in with my work boots on and getting involved in the banter. Everyone knew me and still thought of me as the football kid, even though I was no longer a teenager, no longer played and the long curly hair had all gone. As long as it got me acceptance I didn't care.

I'd always loved music and started DJing alongside Gary on his pirate radio station, SubJam on 104.7. We played house and garage music and quickly grew in popularity. SubJam started taking over nights at clubs and selling them out. I could find myself at Rudolph's, attached to Tottenham's White Hart Lane stadium, not with my boot bag, but with my record bag, ready to DJ for a room of clubbers. Soon enough, I was DJing at Opera House on Tottenham High Road, Warehouse on Edmonton Industrial Estate, Aquarium on Old Street, Sky in Hertfordshire and many others.

I added to my labouring job by selling fireworks, setting up Christmas tree pitches all over Enfield, running markets in Bovingdon and Wembley selling counterfeit goods – mainly fake Nike trainers, Evisu jeans and hair straighteners – and also normal clothes which we'd get from big trucks and warehouses. I even ran my own window cleaning company with my mate in Hoddesdon, which lasted for about a month. I was running around all over the place trying to set up deals and keep my cash flow coming to fund my weekend blowouts.

I was behind the counter of my fireworks shop when my mobile rang. Unknown number. There was nobody in the shop and so I put the phone to my ear.

"Hello?"

"'Ello Sonny." That northern drawl was instantly recognisable. "It's Sam. I'm in Bolton and I'm interested in getting you up here." I was in total shock. Big Sam Allardyce, manager of Premier League club Bolton on the phone. He must have been able to tell I was a little speechless because after a few seconds of silence he carried on. "Are you fit?"

"Not really." I found my voice. It had been months since the whole Grimsby situation, and even more months since I'd actually played a game. Big Sam took it all in his stride.

"Do yourself a favour, then. Get yourself fit and let me know when you're ready. Give me a call and I'll get someone to come down and bring you back up to Bolton so you can train with us."

I put down the phone proper buzzing. I hadn't felt like this about football in years. A Premier League team was interested in me! There could be no greater incentive. In that moment I vowed to get fit, to do everything I could to impress Bolton.

As luck would have it, my mate Sav Kamil's uncle had recently taken over a semi-professional club down the road called Leytonstone FC. He'd been badgering me to come down for a while and now seemed to be the perfect time. The plan was simple. I'd do a bit of training, get match fit, give Big Sam a call back and then impress on trial.

I popped round Terry's house to tell him the good news. There was a knowing look in his eye. After all, it had been him who had engineered the discussion in the first place. All of those agents that I'd had over the years, and yet I'd now been offered trials through a fellow labourer and one of my oldest, most trusted friends who doubled up as my former coach. It turned out he'd been on a golf day with Big Sam and mentioned my name. Sam remembered me and that's how the whole trial had come about. "Show them what you've got, Sonny," he encouraged.

Half-an-hour down the A10 then round the A406 lay Leytonstone's stadium. I drove down for my first training session full of confidence and ambition. I was going to get back to my best. I stepped out of the car willing to succeed and not long after I was ready to get back into my car. I'd already been banging my motor all over the holes and dents of the gravel car park as I pulled to a stop, and as I walked closer to the stadium I began to see more of the differences of non-league football. There was a muddy training pitch to the left of the complex and then the even muddier stadium pitch, though there wasn't much of a stadium. It was more a pitch surrounded by advertising boards with a clubhouse on one side. It wasn't even anywhere near Enfield Town standard. It was a culture shock, totally different to what I'd been used to. In the changing rooms I was introduced to my new team-mates. They were proper working men, some of them puffing on cigarettes, others coming in with their work boots still on and treating the football environment just like their working one.

In all honesty, it freaked me out a bit.

I'd only ever experienced academy or kids' football. A few Barnet reserves games aside, I'd barely kicked a ball in anger in the men's game. The difference was startling. Physically, it was almost incomparable. My new team-mates huffed and puffed, grafted and got stuck in. In terms of technical ability I felt I was in a different class to them, but in terms of bollocks and bite I was miles off.

I stuck with it, attempting to convince myself it'd get better once I got fit. I'd wrap my towel around my face in the changing rooms to cover myself from their cigarette smoke and then sit with them in the bar afterwards as they drunk their pints and waited for their wage packets and information about that Saturday's game. It was tough but I managed another week. Then another. But by the end of the month I was done. It hadn't got better. Football wasn't anything like the game I remembered playing as a kid. It was filled with anxiety, doubt and obligation. It wasn't fun. Training felt like a chore. The game felt like a job.

I stopped going to Leytonstone. For months afterwards I'd scroll through the contacts list in my phone and hover over Sam Allardyce's name. Should I? Shouldn't I? What did I have to lose?

What was the point?

I never did call him back.

I'd always regret it.

19: Goodfella

With no football there was no direction. I was in a new environment, out of my element, and waiting for something new to happen. That's when I decided to spend more time with Mum's boyfriend. Joey Simms had first arrived in Mum's life a few months after the *Coaching and Poaching* saga. He strolled in wearing this great big Barbour jacket, the kind that farmers usually wear. He was short and stocky with hair slowly receding, an East Ender just like my dad.

We began to see more and more of him. My home life was changing just as football was fading away. There was so much change in every aspect. Looking back, it's no wonder I couldn't cope as a 14-year-old.

But Mum was happy and that was what was most important. It had been a long time since her and Dad were together and so I was willing to give this new bloke a chance. One day he sat me down and told me: "I'll never be your dad but I'll be your mate." That earned my respect.

He turned up to watch me play for Loughton and then joined in with the dads v lads game that took place afterwards. It was weird having a different 'Dad' but I let him get on with it. That big Barbour jacket of his flapped around as he chased after the ball. He was totally clueless, slipping left and right on the turf in his jeans and Reebok Classics. If my actual Dad had been there, I thought, he would have been very similar. There was no doubt the pair were cut from the same cloth, both clueless about football, both hard men from the East End willing to get on with it.

"You know, I didn't get on with my mum either," he told me one day. "I had a difficult upbringing. I don't speak to my mum anymore." Just like me and Dad. A shared past. I prodded and probed and he told me why. "When I was growing up she used to embarrass me on purpose. Sometimes she'd dress me up as a girl and take me out in public. Other times she'd lock me in the cupboard under the stairs where she kept the coal. There were mice and rats running around but I wanted to show her I wasn't scared. Whenever she locked me in that cupboard I'd grab onto a couple of them and bite off their heads. Then I'd leave the heads outside the door so she knew that I wasn't scared."

After 18 months, Joe moved into our house on Willow Road. My sisters had gone by then and so it was just the three of us. It was weird to have a new constant presence. Not necessarily a bad thing, just different.

He told us all that he was a builder. I never actually saw him doing any building work – not even in the house – but he had shed loads of tools. Literally. I always had him down as a wheeler dealer, a proper Del Boy. I'd look at him and see a bit of a lump but nothing more.

Then the cars started arriving. Before long, he was going through cars like they were going out of fashion – from tiny Vauxhall Corsas when money was tight to Mercedes jeeps parked outside the front door. One minute he could have plenty of money, the next he could be struggling. Sometimes he'd come home with bin liners full of fifties and count them all out on the kitchen table. There were tens of thousands of pounds there. Money on the table, on the floors, spilling over the sides. "What's your maths like?" he asked me. When I told him I could add and subtract he asked me to help him count it. He once gave me £500 from the pile just for helping. It took several hours in the dead of night, and the next day I went straight down to a clothes shop to spend it all on designer labels.

I knew something wasn't right. I just couldn't put my finger on what. And because we were getting on well I didn't like to ask too many questions.

A short while after passing my driving test a top-of-the-range BMW turned up on the drive. There was only one thing on my mind: having a go behind the wheel.

Joey had always said that his cars were insured up in Scotland and that it'd be no problem for me to drive them. I'd be covered. So when I saw that he'd left the keys on the table, I got straight on the phone to my mates.

"Let's go to Lakeside shopping centre," I said. "I'll drive."

It was a buzz. We only went a few miles along the M25 but to be in control of such an incredible car was like nothing I'd ever felt before. I made sure to be as careful as possible. Despite Joey's insistence, I wanted to make sure there were no issues with any insurance.

I only went and got pulled over.

On the way home I was driving in the middle lane of the motorway, well within the limit, when blue lights began flashing in the rear-view mirror. Panic spread through me. My guts clenched. The police pulled me over on to the hard shoulder and made me get out of the BMW and into the back of their car.

They'd pulled me over because I was driving in the middle lane with excessive caution. I should have moved over to the left. That seemed fine so I asked if I could go.

"One minute," the policeman said. "My colleague is just running an insurance check."

Oh god.

The guts clenched even harder. Surely Joey wouldn't lie. Surely the car would have insurance.

It did. The check came back positive and the police let me go, apologising for the inconvenience. Within a couple of minutes I was back crawling along the M25, showing excessive caution in the slow lane. The chat in the car was all about the incident. As my mates carried on with their conspiracy theories, darker thoughts entered my mind. Why did Joey have so many cars? And why was the insurance done up in Scotland? Something didn't make sense. I just couldn't work out what.

I got back to a house full of people, which was often the case. There were always people coming in and out of the house after Joey moved in. He seemed to be an important man. He'd often leave first thing in the morning and come back later at night.

Soon the clues of what was really happening came in their

droves. There was all of the money, the boxes and boxes of Gucci loafers that came and went, Joey's big, confident persona that meant he was never afraid to tell someone if they were being out of order. But as long as the money was coming in and the bills were being paid, as far as Mum was concerned he really was a builder. Criminal mastermind? It didn't make sense. Not the man in my house who always wore his farmer's jacket.

Then the book came out.

A family friend brought it round. "You need to have a read of this," he told me.

I put it in my suitcase for a lads' holiday.

We were heading to Magaluf and the plan was simple: big nights followed by relaxing days at the pool. There was also the small matter of a football tournament. Our hotel was running its own tournament and inviting teams to come forward. We put a team in, imaginatively calling ourselves Enfield and listing our names on the board. Everyone was on the beers early doors. It was far from a traditional tournament. Instead it was lads dressed in swim shorts and trainers getting half cut between games at the bar by the pitch.

There were teams put in from everywhere. After a couple of matches some fellas came over to me. They'd cottoned on to the fact I was Sonny Pike. The news spread like wildfire. Sonny Pike is playing in the tournament. Yeah, that Sonny Pike. The one from the TV.

After that I was the subject of some pretty rough treatment. Lads were slamming me up against the boards and going for my shins. The worst of it was reserved for the final. At times it felt like our opponents weren't even trying to get the ball. It was as if they were playing human pinball with me, bouncing me against all of the pitch's boards.

We won the final and as far as I was concerned that was that. Football is a physical game. Tackles are going to happen. My mates were the same. There was no point in focusing on all that when we had a tournament victory to celebrate. We headed out into the night, ready to celebrate in true style.

The first bar was a great place to start. We had a couple to get us going and then moved on. The group of lads from the final were in the second bar. They clocked us too and after we made eye contact they made their way over, led by a lad with his hair in braids. I was at the bar and could sense their presence. They parked themselves right next to me without saying a word. The tension rose. The sixth sense sparked. "It's going to go off," I whispered to my mate.

There it was. One of them said something. I didn't catch it and, as I turned around, one of them threw a bottle at me. It missed and went crashing into the display of bottles behind the bar. Pandemonium. The two groups were onto one another but the bouncers had the situation clocked sharpish. They were in and then, as they pushed us out of the bar, one of the other group pulled out a stun gun. All of us were shoved onto the street and the lad with the gun was trying to stun me with it. Both groups quickly realised the new situation. Our group against their group. No bouncers. One stun gun. Fight or flight. If I didn't go for it then, I knew that they would. I didn't want to get bashed up but before I'd made my decision one of their group had stormed up to me. He drew his head back and went to headbutt me. I swerved and his forehead went into my left shoulder. Seeing his guard down, I swung and caught him with a hook to the chin. As he fell forward I pulled his shirt over his head to stop him from doing anything else. That was the cue for everyone to pile in.

Then I clocked it. A pool table. With pool cues. I had a new lease of life. I leapt over a table of diners and grabbed a pool cue, then whacked one of the group over the head with it. I managed to fight off a couple but there were too many. I was on the floor and then the chain around my neck had been removed and they were hitting me and kicking me and all sorts.

By the end of it there was blood on my shirt and my mates were asking if I was okay. The police had got involved and seeing the blood they then made a move for me. "English!" I yelled, holding out both arms as if to prove my innocence. "Not drunk," I added for good measure. It didn't help matters. They whacked me anyway and so I pelted. They chased after me. I thought I was getting away. I thought I could outrun them. Then all of a sudden I was back on the tarmac. One of them had managed to trip me and as I rolled around in pain they began hitting me with their batons.

Even in Magaluf I couldn't escape my name.

And once again look where it got me.

The pool proved a welcome respite from all of the madness. A chance to relax and forget everything. Settled into my sun lounger, I opened the book and my eyes almost popped out of my head. It was called *Untouchables: Dirty Cops, Bent Justice and Racism in Scotland Yard* – and there was Joey's name, right there in print. It was unmistakeable. I read on as the book laid bare Joey's rap sheet.

"Fucking hell, you seen what this geezer is like?" I exclaimed to my mates, showing them the pages, each one making my life seem even crazier than before. I hadn't thought that was possible. There was all sorts of information covered: grasses, police officers, court cases. The main one with Joey was the robbery. There'd been an article in the *Daily Telegraph* that outlined corruption in the Flying Squad of the 1990s and described Joey as one of two "very tough robbers". This, though, was something else. The book went on to describe how Joey strapped a dummy bomb to an accomplice's chest. There were details of all of the major criminals Joey associated with.

"After expenses had been taken out, Simms got £400,000 from a total robbery of £1,300,000."

Wow.

The geezer wasn't just a bit dodgy. He certainly wasn't a builder or a farmer. He was a proper criminal.

"The officers could pretend that they did not know the identities of the other two robbers and hope to gather evidence against them over the next few days or weeks. But the pair were ruthless and clever, and it was thought that they would leave little or no evidence to justify prosecution."

I didn't know whether to be damning of him or in awe.

In the end, I chose the latter.

The sums involved were massive. Even though what he was doing was illegal, it was still impressive. He'd obviously stolen a lot of money over the years. All those bin liners and flash cars now made sense.

When I returned to Enfield I saw him in a different light. Mum must have recognised the change in me because I'd often hear her begging Joey to not let me go out with him. "Don't you dare," she'd say. "Don't you dare take my son with you." She saw the danger with both eyes. A young, impressionable kid with his dream in tatters and a father out of the picture, looking to cling to a new role model and a new life.

And she was right. After returning from holiday I'd ask Joey if I could go out with him in the daytime. Mum wasn't there the first time I asked. I clocked Joey in the front room and asked him where he was going.

"Can I come?" I asked. Joey checked Mum wasn't about and then nodded. I couldn't have been more excited.

Our trips together became more regular. Over time, his way of life became normal. When I wasn't labouring or mucking around in pubs I'd be with Joey. We'd drive around the East End together. Occasionally we'd head into the West End but mainly it was around the areas that Joey knew best. He visited all sorts of people. There was the Big Fella, Little Legs, Barry the Blade, Irish. Bar owners, cafés, corner shops, all of them usually fronts for something else.

The first stop on each patrol would usually be to a guy who owned a shop in East London. I always had to wait in the car at first. Once they'd chatted about whatever they needed to then I was allowed in. The shop masqueraded as a DVD shop but didn't have many customers. And any customers who were there clearly weren't in the market for DVDs.

Early on I was allowed to take some of the pirated DVDs for myself so I could sell them on for profit. When I managed that, I was allowed to progress onto something harder.

Viagra.

There were rows upon rows of it behind the counter. There must have been tens, maybe hundreds of thousands of the pills in his gaffe.

I took a few hundred of the pills and offered them around the pubs of Enfield. When they got snapped up quickly I returned to Hackney for more, also picking up a load of Viagra gels. I soon developed a reputation. I was still known as "the kid who played football" but now I was also "the bloke who can get you cheap Viagra; three for twenty quid".

"Get him a stiff drink," my mates would laugh. "He thinks he's so hard." I laughed along with them. The banter reminded me of the football days.

People came in search of me. It seemed Enfield was a hotbed for erectile dysfunction. With business booming, I got a mate from my footballing past involved. Like me, he knew there was good money in living like Joe. Like me, he was in a transition period of not knowing where to turn. And like me, he soon started to make a decent living, hiding his money in a CD case in his bedroom.

When I was told that one particular fella was in search of

me my heart skipped a beat. I knew who the fella was. He was a local hard man. In all likelihood, he was probably in the same line of work as Joey. I kept one eye open after that as I went about my work. Which was just as well, because a few weeks later he was standing there in front of me.

"That Viagra gel you're selling. I want three grand's worth."

My eyes popped out of my head. All sense of caution was gone. Three grand, just for selling some Kamagra gel! At the mark up I was giving, that meant about £1,500 worth of profit. My head was spinning. The fella told me where to take the gel and when to meet him. I noted it all down, then went back to Hackney to get as many of the pills as I could.

On the day of the drop off I stuffed a gym bag full of Kamagra. 'Imagine if I get pulled over looking like this,' I thought. 'It's going to look right dodgy.'

The journey over took longer than expected. I didn't dare risk detection so I went down the side streets, doing my best to stay scarce.

"Ha, what you got there, son? Looks like a drug delivery," the man on the door laughed as I walked into the meeting place. Adrenaline surged through me as I tried to laugh it off. In truth I was scared stiff. But as long as he didn't look inside the bag I knew I'd be fine. The man on the door carried on laughing and stepped aside to let me in. I breathed a huge sigh of relief.

The fella was standing in reception, waiting with the money. He led me into a side room which was decorated with crossed swords on the wall. A warning. I opened the gym bag and showed him the gel. He counted it out, then when he was happy he counted out the money. I stuffed it back into my gym bag and thanked him for his custom. We shook hands and then went our separate ways. I tried to remain casual as I walked out, defying the urge to break into a jog in case he changed his mind.

The buzz was incredible as I walked back out of those same doors and thanked the same man on the door. I'd made my first big deal. This was the life.

It was easy money, good money.

20: Hard Up

Once you get a buzz, you want to repeat the feeling over and over again. Now I had my new buzz. After my Viagra deal I promised to dedicate more time to my wheeling and dealing. I'd spend more time patrolling with Joey. I'd meet more people and deal with new clients in the East End.

I was still labouring but it was taking up less of my time. The money coming in from Joey's work was good – more than enough for a 21-year-old. And so instead of labouring from Monday to Friday it was now a case of working whenever I was needed. I could be selective. When an opportunity to work on a roof of the house six doors down for £50 cash in hand came about I jumped at the chance.

"You're the only guy who could get a job one minute away from where he lives!" the lads on the site laughed. They were merciless in their mickey-taking but I didn't mind. While they were all slogging through the traffic on their way back home I'd be on the sofa with my feet up.

The location was great. I could nip back to Mum's house whenever I fancied. Late starts and early finishes were a godsend. And if anyone ever knocked on the front door I could call to them from my position on the roof to let them know where I was. Joey came and went, as ever, but he could also be seen walking our dog, Boss, every now and again. It was hard to miss the pair of them. The dog was almost the size of a horse, a great big French mastiff, a Dogue de Bordeaux. You wouldn't mess with Joey, but when he had that dog on a lead there was absolutely no way anyone in their right mind would mess with him.

Sometimes Joey would spot me and we'd acknowledge each other. Often he just went about the task at hand, the horse-dog pulling him along without a care in the world.

I was standing in the apex roof looking out at the street when it happened. Joey was walking the dog as always. The farmer's jacket was zipped up to the top. Everything seemed right with the world. I stopped knocking my nails into wood and watched the pair of them make their way towards Mum's house. I watched as they turned the corner onto Willow Road. I watched as 20 policemen came from nowhere and charged at them. I watched as Joey stopped in his tracks. I watched as he let them handcuff him.

Jesus.

People came out of their houses to watch. "They're nicking him! They're nicking him!"

"Bloody hell!" the lads on the site screamed as they all stopped what they were doing. They couldn't believe it. Nor could I.

None of them knew my relationship with Joey. None of them knew that what was happening was horrifying. It was only the boss, Chris Osborn, who had any inkling.

"That's your house, isn't it?" he asked.

"Yeah it is."

"And your stepdad? Go and do what you gotta do."

I raced off that roof as sharp as I could. They were putting Joey in their police car by the time I got there. He'd gone quietly.

"Give us a hand and put that dog of yours in the garden," one of the policemen said. They all knew exactly who I was. They'd been monitoring the comings and goings at Willow Road for a long time.

I took our dog in a trance. "Come straight back!" the police ordered as I opened the front door. I left him in the garden and as I re-entered the house I could hear the police shouting through the letterbox. They were becoming paranoid that I was racing around the house destroying evidence.

"Come back! We need you to open the door right now!"

A rage built up inside me. Why should I open the door and let these strangers into my territory? I hovered at the door, refusing to open it.

"Get this fucking idiot out of the way," the lead policeman, a tall blond officer, shouted. They could all see me through the letterbox.

"Prick," I replied. I was wound up. I didn't care what they thought. Let them arrest me. Let them do whatever.

Whoosh.

The door was forced open and I was pushed back against the wall.

The police officers charged in and set about searching the property. A handful of them set up base at the kitchen table while the rest made off with transparent bags to find evidence.

The reality of the situation took hold. I couldn't exactly fight off 20 policemen and order them out of my house. Gingerly, I got up and made my way to the kitchen table. I was still so shocked about the whole thing.

"What's up?" the policeman at the table asked. "Are you not used to something like this?"

"No. Not at all."

"I thought you would be. We do this kind of thing day in, day out."

Two weeks later I found out from an estate agent mate of mine how the police had been renting a house just down the street from us for six months to monitor Joey's activity. They'd even managed to set up a camera inside our porch. They knew all there was to know about Mum and me.

It didn't half put me off selling my counterfeit goods and Viagra. That could have been me. Not necessarily with what I was dealing in, but if I'd moved onto the next stage then I could have been the one in the back of a police car.

Eventually, the police left. They couldn't find anything but still locked Joey up on remand.

The house was a quiet place. I sat there alone at the kitchen table, trying to register all that had just happened. Mum was shocked when she returned home, but at the same time she wasn't. She'd always turned a blind eye to Joey's dealings and tried to believe he really was builder, a car dealer, a ducker and diver. In reality, she had her suspicions. We all did.

21: Back to Amsterdam

Joey was remanded for six months until his court case started. We visited him regularly in Belmarsh, his Category A, high-security prison in Thamesmead, south-east London.

The sheer scale of it was incredible. On my first visit I looked around in awe. There must have been at least 50 visitors allowed at any one time. They were all sitting around these small tables in a room that wouldn't have looked out of place as a sports hall, waiting for the prisoners to enter. Each table had four chairs, three on one side and one on the other. A door in the corner of the room opened and out trudged the inmates. They were all wearing bright bibs. Orange bib. Orange bib. Orange bib. You couldn't miss the prisoners. Orange bib. Orange bib. Orange bib. Green bib.

What?

Why was Joey in a green bib when everyone else was in orange? A guard took Joey's name and showed us to the table where we were seated.

"He's taking it well," the guard told us. "This breaks many of our prisoners. Joey has stayed strong."

That made us all feel better.

"All right?" I didn't know what else to say to him. Joey greeted us all and I asked why he was in the green bib.

"It's because of my past convictions with explosives, which means they treat me as if I'm a terrorist. They also think there's a high chance of me breaking out due to the people they associate me with."

The highest risk in a Category A prison? A place where people like Great Train Robber Ronnie Biggs and hate preacher Abu Hamza were also locked up? The man in the farmer's jacket who'd lived in my house for the best part of a decade? It was mad. Absolutely mad.

We carried on visiting. Over time we got to know the other prisoners and their families. Ronnie Biggs would usually be wearing a T-shirt with a picture of a £50 note, the Queen's face and his name on it underneath the orange bib. Visitors would ask for pictures with him and all sorts. Joey saw it all and got on with it. He'd introduce us to some of the other prisoners, too. There was a system where the inmates would ask their visitors to go and buy food or drink for fellow prisoners. Joey used to ask me to grab extra waters, sweets and snacks from the canteen for the visits. He wasn't allowed to go and get them so it fell upon me. I'd run the errand and then drop the Jaffa Cakes with the prisoners Joey directed me towards. "Nice one, son," they'd say.

"Who's that?" I asked Joey of one of the recipients.

"That's one of the guys who done the Millennium Dome raid, the one where they tried to snatch the diamonds and run off on a speedboat."

£350 million worth of diamonds, to be exact.

The next errand Joey asked me to run was on another level, to say the least. "You remember that weekend you had in Amsterdam?" he asked. How could I forget? Joey had put me and my mate Jamie up for the weekend while I was getting involved in the Viagra dealing. Joey used to go out to Holland every now and again, doing whatever it was that he did, and said we were welcome to come and stay while he went about his business.

Me and Jamie were met at the airport by Joey and three of his friends. The geezers looked like trouble, proper dodgy. Jamie gave me a nervous look and whispered: "Sonny, what have you got me involved in here?" Even I was a little bit shocked.

They took us to the flat they were staying in, about 45 minutes from the centre of Amsterdam. There were loads of family photos up on the walls, all the same family, yet none of them in the flat itself. "What's going on?" I asked one of the friends. "Who are all these people?"

"When your stepdad comes out here we tell this family they have to leave for a few days so he can stay," he replied.

On the first night we all went out into Amsterdam together. It was just like we were back in London, making our way around the bars and caffs that his associates used as fronts for their line of work. Each one would welcome Joey with open arms and then give us whatever we wanted for free. It was as if we had this magic carpet around the city.

"I'm heading out for a couple of hours," Joey told us. There were a couple of Indian restaurants that he owned and wanted to check up on, as well as a pub he was looking to buy. "Don't do anything stupid." Straight away, we went and did something stupid. Me and Jamie went on to have a proper mad weekend. He'd been doing drugs for a long time whereas I was still relatively new to it. I took my first load of magic mushrooms in Amsterdam. They initially had no effect and so we went back and consumed a second load that were stronger. We didn't realise they took a bit of time to get into your system and they sent us off our trolleys. We were wandering around Amsterdam, walking along a zebra crossing but every time I got to the end of it the crossing came again, and again, and again. It was never-ending, just like an escalator. "What's going on?" I asked Jamie. "Don't worry," he replied. "You're just tripping." We jumped in a taxi and the driver was wearing a leather jacket which made him look like he was melting into the leather seat. "Are you seeing this?" I demanded of Jamie.

But at Belmarsh, Joey wasn't referring to our mad weekend. Not the drugs part, anyway. It was one of the friends.

"You remember the lad you didn't get on with?" he asked. Of course I did. On our travels around Amsterdam I had a heated argument with him that almost ended in a fight. I didn't like the way he acted and felt there was something funny about him, something not right. At the time, Joey told me to leave it. He didn't want me to get into a fight with one of his business connections. But now things were different. Now, he suspected the man was a grass.

"Find out as much as you can about him," Joey said. "You

know the place where I hide my money? Go there and take out enough for your flight and expenses. Go to Amsterdam and find him. Find out as much as you can." With that he handed me a scrunched up piece of paper. "Here's the area where the flat that you stayed in is located. Find this flat and find this man. He'll put you on the right path. He'll sign a witness statement too. He's a good bloke."

I didn't think twice. After leaving Joey I went to his hiding place and took out enough money to run my latest errand. I felt like I owed him. Joey had always looked after me, from giving me £20 every day to cover my food and travel when I was at Stevenage to more recently, when he'd opened my eyes to a new line of business.

One of Joey's contacts met me at Amsterdam airport and put me up in his place on the outskirts of the city. That was my base. I'd sleep there, then spend the rest of my time scouring the streets.

The irony wasn't lost on me. After all these years I was back in Amsterdam. No longer the child superstar, England's brightest footballer, but instead trying to hunt down a suspected supergrass while attempting to stay on the right side of the law.

Each day I'd search an area of Amsterdam, the crumpled piece of paper I held in my pocket my guide. That rough area was all I knew about the place I was looking for. It wasn't much to go off. And yet after two days of searching I found it. I knew it was the right place. I remembered the building from our mad weekend. Yes, it was definitely the place.

Walking up the stairs to the flat, my nerves started to build up. What was I doing? What if they made the link between me and Joey, then made the link to what had happened to Joey, and things got nasty? What if I caught them at the worst possible time? And what would they think to a skinny 22-year-old demanding answers to secrets they wanted to keep secret. There could be trouble at best.

A man answered the door. He was short and middle aged with dark hair. He wasn't one of Joey's main connections. I hadn't met him before. Yet nor was he the man from all of the family photos that were still on the walls. By now I was scared. Things could so easily go wrong. I willed myself to stay calm, to stay focused.

"Hello?"

I told the man who I was and who I was looking for. When the man didn't react badly I went on to tell him Joey's suspicions that one of his business connections was a supergrass. I asked if it was true.

"There's a good chance your dad is right," the man replied. Joey's connections often referred to him as my dad and I never bothered to put them right. "He's been in prison many times and we know he plays both sides of the law. Tell Joe I wouldn't be surprised if it's true."

I asked where the suspected supergrass was but my question couldn't be answered. The man promised to keep a look-out and let me know if anything changed. The only thing left for me to do was to ask for a witness statement, which the man was happy to sign. It said that Joey had only been in Amsterdam because he wanted to buy a bar in the

Red Light District, which was actually true. The man was happy to sign the document. "Whatever Joey needs of me, I'll do," he promised.

I left the flat with a huge amount of relief. My mission was over. It hadn't ended in disaster. I'd found out valuable information. I'd got the statement. That was the end of it as far as I was concerned.

Whether it really was the end of it, though, I never found out.

***

When the court case started it was conducted at Belmarsh prison. Due to the perceived high risk of a breakout, they didn't want to move Joey if they didn't have to.

Me and Mum went every day, intrigued but nervous. We sat in the spectators' gallery above the court room. There were thick bullet-proof glass screens everywhere in that court room. It was the best way to prevent violence, sectioning everyone off from each other. The jury members were seated below the defendant so they couldn't even see each other. The risk of a high-category prisoner recognising a jury member and seeking revenge wasn't one worth taking.

Joey was one of four defendants. They'd all been brought to trial as part of the same elaborate scheme. The judge broke down the case for all of those present and I couldn't help but be impressed by the audacity of Joey. The sums involved were big, the operation mind-blowing. Over three weeks we heard how the four of them had worked with people in Holland, who had also all been nicked, to obtain stolen goods. Stolen paintings, apparently, totalling millions of pounds.

It was the phone records that really went against him. All of the drug dealers and shady characters in the crime ring had one thing in common: Joey's phone number at the centre of all activity. We watched on as the lawyer showed footage of one of the crime ring in the back of a lorry. There were paintings and antiques from Iraq in the lorry but, most importantly, there were Class A drugs with a street value of millions.

Joey watched on then turned to me and Mum. He looked up at us as the judge summarised the evidence and he tied an imaginary noose around his neck. He knew he was done.

Guilty.

Two weeks later he was sentenced. As far as I was concerned it was a formality and so Mum decided it was best to go to the court by herself.

My head had gone. I was gutted.

I'd thought he was untouchable.

Nothing could have prepared me for Mum's phone call later that day. I was fitting a kitchen on Kings Avenue in Muswell Hill when my phone rang.

They gave him 22 years.

22: Rock Bottom

Every time I was onto a good thing it got taken away. Football, father figures, acting, even the media appearances. So many promising starts and failed endings. My life was one big failure. That's all that I could think about.

I was past caring.

Before Joey was locked up I was mucking about in pubs and doing stupid stuff. Drinking in the week, drugs at the weekend. I'd never go in search of drugs but if they were there then I'd get involved. And with my mates they sometimes were. Soon enough it became a normal thing in the same way that people puff on cigarettes when they're drunk.

Then Joey was **in prison** and there seemed no other way to turn. I was lost. There was nothing to look forward to anymore. Nothing on my mind. No plans. Just drink and drugs and living for the weekend.

The night before Christmas Eve, a group of my mates headed over to Shepherd's Bush for a school disco night. We were all dressed up in mock school uniform, unbuttoned shirts and wonky ties all over the place. In the queue we had a big bottle of vodka which we challenged ourselves to finish before getting to the front. We were passing it around and encouraging each other on, making each other drink a certain amount of fingers, knocking the straight vodka straight down. The competitive spirit fired up. I was going to drink more than anyone else.

By the time we got to the front of the queue we were all proper drunk. Not drunk enough to be refused entrance but drunk enough to not really be in control. We got into the club and it was wicked. The place was busy and had a large stage area at the front where people could dance. Clubbers were queuing up at one side of the stage, dancing for a song, then exiting on the other side to let the next set of people on. That looked right up our street. We managed a few more drinks at the bar then headed over to the queue, ready to strut ourselves around on stage.

A group of lads joined the queue. Standing immediately behind us, they were obviously as drunk as we were. They were loud, forceful and had little awareness of personal space. I suppose me and my mates were the same.

I don't know how the argument broke out. It could have been them pushing in front of us, it could have been us reacting to their provocations. But once the argument started, it wasn't long until it went further. Pushes were coming in at every angle. Then punches. Before I knew it there was a full-scale brawl going on and I was falling down the stairs and dragging someone else with me.

The bouncers were in quickly. They grabbed as many of us as they could and dragged us all into a side room. That was odd. Usually you get thrown out of the club, not moved into a side room. We soon found out why. The club was located next door to a police station. Whenever the club had any trouble they gave their neighbours a call.

It was all getting too much. Two police officers entered the side room. "What's going on here," they asked the club owner. He told them about the fight and the police looked in the direction of one of the other group of lads. He'd been hurt pretty badly and was covered in blood.

"Do you want to press charges?"

Jesus.

"Where's the CCTV footage?" they asked the club owner. This was quickly becoming serious. It wasn't just being treated as a routine scrap in a nightclub.

The police led me and my mates out of the side room and into the prison cells next door. We weren't interviewed because we were all far too drunk and barely made any sense. Instead, we were each given our own cell. It was as basic as you like. A blue mattress that was impossibly thin. A toilet. A window.

The situation hadn't hit home. We chose to fight it. The doors each had a little peephole and we were all opening them and shouting out at each other and giving it the big 'un and singing along to Oasis songs such as *Morning Glory*. For a good half-hour we were embracing it all. But eventually it wound down into silence. People became tired. A reaction didn't come. The peepholes closed. We were each alone.

Alone in prison with silence all around. It's enough to drive you crazy. From a cell opposite I heard a banging. It was one of my mates. He couldn't take being locked up and so he was trying to do something about it. He was charging up to the walls and headbutting them. When that didn't do anything he tried to suffocate himself.

Fucking hell.

"Do something!" I yelled. "Get down here! You've got to come and help. He's trying to hurt himself."

The police officer on duty rushed down and calmed my mate down. They promised to keep an eye on him for the rest of the night.

The excitement was over. The silence was back. I did sit-ups and press-ups to pass the time but soon enough I was sitting on my bed and staring at the ceiling, looking into the nothingness.

What was I doing?

I was in a cell, obviously, but what was I doing? What was I doing with my life? How could I be in a cell on Christmas Eve?

For the first time in a long time, I had the chance to stop and think. With no distractions, no constant blur around me and just the silence of prison, memories came flooding back. Memories that I tried to suppress and had been gone for months, years. I thought back to my life in football. The early press, Ajax, the comparisons to Best and Giggs and Shearer, the promise, the potential, the nothingness. I thought of Terry and smiled. I thought of the documentary and cursed. I had the world at my feet. I had all of those chances. Such a bright future. And look where I'd got to.

I lay down on my tiny mattress and carried on looking

up at the ceiling. The memories kept coming. There was Loughton and Palace and QPR. There were the hours up in my loft, refusing to go out into the outside world. There was Archway. I thought back to the sheer drop and the urge to end it all.

I didn't jump but I couldn't go much lower than my current situation. I was in a cell. Joey was in a cell. That was the path I was on. If I didn't fix up I'd be just like Joey. He was banged up for 22 years. I'd done two hours and it was more than enough. Horrible. One of the worst experiences of my life.

I couldn't take that path.

I had to sort myself out. Turn my life around. Get off the drink and drugs. Stop living for the rush, as if every day was my last.

It had all gone too far.

I was the last of my mates to be released. We had the interview and I responded "no comment" to every question – mainly because I was so hungover that I really couldn't remember what had happened. The police then allowed me one phone call. I used it on Mum. I could hear the panic in her voice when I told her what had happened. I didn't like it. I begged her to get me out of the place as soon as possible. It'd be Christmas Day in a few hours. I wanted to spend it with my family.

Mum hung up and got straight on the phone to Rosie.

23: Rosie

I hadn't known Rosie long but it had been enough time to know she was special. As chaos rained down all around, she was the positive, my straight and narrow.

She was waiting outside the police station in her black Ford Fiesta. I walked toward her in the darkness. They'd taken my clothes when I was brought in and I was still in the paper-thin boiler suit they'd given me. I stunk. I hadn't showered in days. I didn't have any money on me.

"Can you lend me a tenner?"

I looked like a tramp. Yet she saw the desperation in my eyes and reached into her purse. She waited in the car while I went to Tesco to get something to eat, faithful as ever, still smiling when I got back into the car, still chatty as she took me to Mum's house.

It was that smile that first attracted me. I'll never forget the day, 10 September 2006, shortly before my 23rd birthday. Keeley, the girlfriend of my mate Gary, pulled up at my house with a car full of girls. I bounced over and peered into the back of her car to see this big beaming smile. It caught my eye and so I looked straight at the girl and saw her big, blue eyes shining back. I found myself staring and staring.

She was beautiful. "Come on," I said. "You're coming in with me."

Everyone in the car was coming with me. They'd arrived to come into my house and enjoy the barbecue I was putting on to celebrate my birthday. That didn't seem important right then. Only one thing seemed important.

She didn't come straight away and so I opened the door and gently took her by the wrist. I'd had a couple of drinks and was feeling more confident than usual. It worked. Rosie followed me into the house, slightly nervous but still beaming.

I spoke to her for the whole night. I wanted to find out everything there was to know. She told me about her horses, the work she did with her dad at their family stables in Crews Hill, her friends, her showjumping, the knee replacement she'd needed after a riding accident, the months of school she had missed as a result, the bad back injury that put an end to her showjumping and required her spine to be fused and pins in her side, everything. In turn I told her about my life. I told her about my family, my mates, my work. Every detail – apart from the massive football chunk, which I made sure to leave out. She didn't need to know that. I didn't need to bring back those old memories.

When she left, I couldn't wait to see her again.

I had to wait a week. We were celebrating another mate's birthday and, once again, Gary brought Keeley and Keeley brought her mates, including Rosie. I didn't even consider playing it cool. Instead, I made a beeline for her. We got chatting at the bar, carrying on exactly from where we left off the week before.

"Rosie really likes you."

I turned around. It was Keeley. She was standing behind me with the drink she'd just ordered. I had a quick minute to talk to her while Rosie wasn't there.

"Does she?" I asked. I wanted to hear Keeley say it again.

"She really likes you," Keeley confirmed. It was exactly what I wanted to hear.

At the end of the night I took Rosie's number and from that moment the messages started.

I offered to pick her up and then take her into town for food and a drink. When I arrived, however, it wasn't just Rosie. Her older sister Cara was also there. It turned out that Rosie was just 17 years old, five years younger than me. I'd thought she was the same age as me but it wasn't a big deal. I'd already fallen for her.

Cara chaperoned her for the whole night. Rosie must have been nervous before I arrived, maybe a little apprehensive, but she soon opened up with that great big beaming smile. I took them to The George first, my regular pub in Enfield. That turned out to be a bit of a mistake. We got ourselves a table and a few drinks, but every half-hour another of my mates would turn up. 'Steady on,' I was thinking. I knew how easily my mates could take things too far but fortunately Rosie embraced it all. She laughed along with them but never took her eyes far off me.

After our food we moved on to the other bars and pubs of Enfield and had a good night. When I finally put Rosie and

Cara into a taxi home to Crews Hill we agreed we had to do it all over again. I must have left a good impression because Cara was nowhere to be seen on our next date. This time it was just the two of us. I knew I had to take her somewhere more intimate, where my mates wouldn't turn up and stare. Fortunately, I had the perfect solution: Nando's.

That second date turned into a third date, a fourth date, a fifth date. When Rosie went into hospital for more surgery on her back, it seemed a make-or-break moment. For two weeks she remained in the BUPA hospital over in Bushey. I visited her every day, using Victoria's house move to Watford as the perfect excuse. I'd help Victoria in the day and then see Rosie in the evening. Sometimes Victoria would come with me, other times Mum would. It showed Rosie that I cared. We weren't official, but after those two weeks we might as well have been.

I received plenty of stick from my mates down the pub. As much as I was seeing Rosie, I was still spending plenty of time with my mates though. They soon welcomed her into the group when they found out how useful it was to have someone who didn't drink. Rosie had never really been into nights out and so she assumed the role of driver, taking us from one place to another. Often, she'd also have to be our getaway driver when things turned nasty.

Despite my promise to turn my life around, the drinking was still spiraling dangerously close to being out of control. So much so that one night it all almost came crashing down. We started off as usual in The George and then moved on into town. The drinks were flowing and we were far from the only group of lads who'd had a few too many. Banter soon got out of hand. Another group were eyeing us up. Then they jumped in and everyone was fighting. I threw a few punches and gave as good as I got before we were all split up.

The next morning I woke up in agony. Rosie, lying next to me in bed, insisted that I go to the hospital to get it looked at.

"Leave it out," I told her. I'd be fine. It was just a scratch. The pain would wear off. But there was no changing Rosie's mind.

Not for the first time in our relationship, she was right. Rosie took me to Chase Farm Hospital in Enfield and, when we eventually got around to seeing a doctor later that day, I was told that I'd need an immediate operation. My knuckles had been smashed to bits the previous evening. They wheeled me off and all of a sudden I was in an operating theatre. They inserted five pins into my hand and then sewed me back up.

I was kept in hospital after that and put on a drip. All I could do was lie there in my hospital bed, all wired up to this plastic bag. Talk about bored. I wanted to be out and about, not cooped up in a hospital room with a load of old people.

When Rosie came into the room I told her exactly how I was feeling.

"I've had enough. I need to get out. To get some air."

"You're mad," she replied. "Look at you. You've just had an operation. You need to get some rest."

"Don't worry, I'll come back." It was my turn to be insistent. I took the drip, wires and all, and shoved it into my pocket as best I could. "Let's go to Nando's," I suggested.

I could feel people looking at me as I tucked into my half chicken and chips. They weren't staring because I was Sonny Pike the boy wonder, though. They were staring because there was this mad bloke with a load of wires coming out of his arm and a drip in his pocket.

"You're mad," Rosie repeated over and over, but she did so with a smile. When we finished our meals and paid up I didn't feel like returning to the hospital. I felt fine and didn't fancy the endless hours of staring at the hospital ceiling.

"I can't go back there. Not yet," I told Rosie.

"Okay then," she replied. "Do you want to meet my mum and dad then?"

"All right."

As first impressions go, there have probably been better ones. I was a little nervous as I walked up the driveway to the family home in Crews Hill but nothing too bad. Maybe it was the post-operation drugs that had sedated me. Rosie's mum and dad hid well any shock at the state of their daughter's new boyfriend. No matter their true feelings, they made sure they were all smiles when I walked into the kitchen to say hello. Her dad, Keith, immediately offered his hand for me to shake. I looked at him, then looked at him again. I knew him. Years ago, back when Terry first started training me, he occasionally made me go out for runs. Terry would dress me up in the big army boots and then follow me on his mountain bike as I went about my route. When Terry wasn't about I'd do the route by myself. Whenever I went, I'd always see this bloke in his yard. He'd be doing the trees, mowing the lawn, sorting everything out. After the first few sightings we began to acknowledge each other. Just a little nod of the head, then on I went. It became a little routine. The memories came flooding back as I took Keith's hand and shook it with my uninjured left hand. I'd moved on since all of those years ago while he was still in the same yard, doing the same work. I'd left football after being eaten up, chewed around and spat out. Keith didn't know all of that.

Keith was the perfect gentleman. Though he looked as if he could have been one of Joey's mates – a bit of a handful – he proved to be anything but. He showed me around and Rosie's mum, Jo, offered me food and drink. They were the perfect hosts. And Rosie's whole family life seemed perfect to me. The house was welcoming. They had 68 acres of land for the horses. Tacked on to the main house were a couple of mobile homes. There was space everywhere, both inside and out. Rosie had never told me she lived in such luxury.

I left Rosie's house inspired. The whole way back to the hospital I thought about how good she had it.

After that first visit I kept on going back. Without the drip in my pocket I felt more confident around Rosie's family. I learned all about them. I found out how Rosie worked in the stables with her dad, bringing on the horses he brought over from Ireland to sell on. I saw how the family cared for as many as 60 horses at a time. I heard about Keith's visits to Ireland to find horses for Rosie. I discovered the shop he'd built for Cara on their site so she could set up her own business. I watched Keith's son, Jack, as he opened a car valeting company. The family would do anything for each other. And what made it all the more impressive was that they were self-made.

Keith had been just like me once. He'd scraped by as a greengrocer before getting into the van business. Creating his own company that bought, sold and hired vans allowed him to diversify into property and horses. Everything they wanted they could have.

The night in the prison cell was a wake-up call. But meeting Keith was the wake-up call that I needed. By that stage Rosie had already put up with a lot. The hand, the drinking, the fights, the trouble. I was lucky she stuck by me. She must have seen something in me.

"Why are you getting yourself into fights for?" Keith asked the next time I went round. "Why are you getting into trouble over nothing? If there was loads of money in it for you then I'd understand but you're doing it for nothing. It's not worth it."

Keith liked to have a drink but knew where his limits were. He was a clued-up businessman. He didn't shout at people and tell them they were worthless. Instead, he was totally down-to-earth.

I listened to his words and found myself agreeing with them. What was I doing? Why was I wasting my time with drink when I could be making something of myself? I vowed to hold back, to never let myself get carried away again. After all, I had a responsibility to Rosie now.

I'm not a religious person but I truly believe I was meant to meet Keith. He was the guidance I needed in wayward times. With his help, I got to the corner and I turned it.

24: Searching

Not long after Christmas, Rosie moved in with me and Mum. She was coming round to ours so much that she brought some spare clothes over. Then a few more. Then most of her stuff. She ended up staying for the best part of six months.

With Rosie and her family's help, I managed to find a balance with my social life. The nights out with my mates continued but I knew when to stop. There was too much to risk.

While Rosie helped me, she struggled to adapt to her new life. I'd always joked with her that she was a carrot muncher, used to a quiet way of life out in the sticks. In reality, she was used to a nice settled home life. Living with the Pikes opened her eyes. She never quite got used to being the only person about in the mornings. Though Joey was gone, our open-door policy remained. There were always people about but only ever in the afternoons and evenings. Money appeared from all sorts of places. Barbecues could go on for three days. Mum liked a night out herself. While Rosie got up, hoovered and walked the dog, the rest of us remained sleeping. It was exactly the kind of lifestyle Rosie had been sheltered from. Wild. And she didn't like it one bit.

The visits to Rosie's family continued. When Mum decided to sell the house on Willow Road and move 15 minutes further into Hertfordshire, I returned the favour to Rosie. The new house would be too small for all of us and so we moved in to Rosie's parents' yard at Crews Hill, living in one of the mobile homes on their land. That was different. You always see your own family as normal until you become close with another family. At Rosie's they all got up in the mornings and went about their tasks. Things were quiet, predictable. At the end of each day they all came together and ate as a family while asking each other about their days. On a Sunday they'd do the same but ask about the week they'd each had and what they had planned for the coming week. It was all so alien to me. I was used to an open house, people coming and going all the time, no organisation, not having a clue what was going on with each other.

I'd laughed at Rosie for being a carrot cruncher but the longer I lived with her the more I enjoyed the organised and stable life.

Seeing Keith in particular go about his work every day only made me more motivated to succeed. I began to build up a character, one who'd prove himself to be just like Keith, only even better. It was a healthy rivalry. I'd see Keith getting up at 6am and so I'd make sure that I was up at 5am. When I'd come back from my day of labouring and see Keith still working around the yard I'd make a point of going for a run. Self-improvement became a priority, and the new structure in my life allowed me to improve my mindset and mental health. I started a chippy course, committing two years of part-time study to give carpentry a go.

I was doing it for myself. I was doing it for Rosie. And then I was given a whole new motivation.

The test came back positive. Rosie was pregnant. I was going to be a father.

Shock. Happiness. Elation.

The time soon came to tell our families. My sister Victoria was first. She was shocked and happy, but mostly excited to see Mum's reaction. I clutched on to a little image I had of the 12-week scan in my pocket as I told Rosie's mum next. She was beaming, just like Rosie had been that first time I met her.

"As long as you two are happy then so am I," she said as she looked once more at the photo of the scan. "But you best tell him now."

Her finger was pointing out into the yard. Keith was out there, going about his business as usual.

"Keith, I've got something to tell you mate."

"What? What's that?" He stopped his work and stood upright, wary of what was to come. It was as if he knew there was something big happening. I reached into my pocket and got out the scan. I pressed it into his hand.

"Nothing bad," I replied.

"Just tell me. Tell me. Tell me." He never liked to be kept in suspense.

"Me and Rosie have got some news."

He stared at the scan, taking it all in. When he looked up, I knew everything was going to be all right.

"Well as long as you and Rosie are happy then I'm happy."

Mum was far less calm when we told her.

"Oh my god, my baby is having a baby!"

"Leave it out, Mum. I'm 25."

"You'll always be my baby. And now you're having a baby. Oh my god!"

Freya Pike was born in Chase Farm Hospital on 24 February 2009 at 3.35am. It was incredible. The length Rosie went to, the strain she put her body under to produce our wonderful daughter, was unbelievable. I was petrified of what was going on. I tried to take Rosie's hand during the birth so I could help her through it but didn't do the best of jobs. My emotions were all over the place. I was so excited. Then when Freya did come out I crumbled, with emotions that I never knew existed going through my body. Great big crocodile tears were running down my cheeks. The nurse asked me to cut the umbilical cord but I was in such a state that I insisted Rosie's mum did it. I could barely stand up.

When Freya finally started crying I felt so much relief. I didn't realise that not all babies cry when they come into this world. The wait was agonising. But when the first wail came I collapsed in happiness. She was alive. My daughter was healthy. Those feelings and emotions that had never been there before continued to surge through my body. The nurse passed her to me and I managed to stay upright as I took her into my arms. I touched her skin, still disbelieving.

The love was instant and unconditional. I wanted to do anything I could to help this human through her life. I sat there, running my hands over her fingers and toes, checking that they were all there. They were. She was perfect. Beautiful. A gift.

When she was removed from my arms I watched as her chest moved up and down. Every breath was a gift. I could have stayed there for hours watching her. But I wasn't allowed to. At 5am I was told that I'd need to leave. So I drove home, had a shower, then drove straight to Greggs. I sat in the car until it opened, then grabbed as much food as I could for Rosie before heading straight back to the hospital. There was no way I was sleeping. There was no chance I was spending any less time than the maximum possible with my daughter.

Life was becoming good again. Every day spent in the company of Rosie, our family and my daughter was a blessing. The bad memories of my past life continued to disappear. There was a light at the end of the tunnel and I was speeding towards it. Everything was becoming lighter. My depression seemed such a long time ago.

Keith gave me motivation. Freya gave me purpose. I drove myself harder than ever, working as many hours as possible so I could provide for my little family. We were still living in the mobile home on Rosie's family's yard and it wasn't enough. We needed a place of our own. My whole focus became on earning enough money so we could sort ourselves out.

I'd passed the chippy course and was getting odd jobs

through, stuff like fitting kitchens, laying floors and putting up fences. The labouring work kept on coming. But it didn't seem enough. Once again I looked at Keith. He didn't rely on anyone else for his work. He was in total control of what he did, a self-employed man made good.

Self-employment. It made sense to me. That way I'd be out on my own with no excuses if it all went wrong. There was no chance I could be misled, just as I had been so many times by so many people with ulterior motives. And after all, I was multi-trained. I had something to offer. I just needed to work out what.

Then one of my mates, Ryan, told me about the Knowledge. He was planning on starting it and becoming a cabbie. 'Yeah', I thought as I listened in. 'I fancy a bit of that.'

An agreement was made. We both bought mopeds and started driving around the streets of London, becoming accustomed to their turns and landmarks. We drove to Knowledge Points on Caledonian Road and bought all of the books we needed for the course. I got a great big map of London too and stuck it on the wall at home. When I wasn't driving around London I was in front of that map, testing myself over and over on street names until they stuck, just like what would happen in the examinations. When it came down to the exams, I'd be asked to say the exact location of two points on the map and then recite the best route between the two places, which they call a run. The better the route chosen, the higher the score. C is a pass; AA is the top mark.

Manor House? That's on Green Lanes.

Gibson Square? That's just off Milner Place, Islington.

The route? Leave on left, Green Lanes, right Brownswood Road, left Blackstock Road, forward Highbury Park, forward Highbury Grove, right St. Paul's Road, comply Highbury Corner, leave by Upper Street, right Islington Park Street, left College Cross, right Barnsbury Street, left Milner Place, forward Milner Square, forward Milner Place, Gibson Square.

Straight to the map. Look at the route just recited. Get in there! The buzz when I got a route right was the closest I'd had to the thrill of scoring a goal. I'd run around the room screaming "yes!" at the top of my lungs. Yet the low when it all went wrong was devastating, absolutely gutting.

I was enjoying learning. It was a slog but fortunately living in the mobile home without a mortgage or bills to pay meant I was able to stick it out. Ryan wasn't so lucky. The pressures of life became too much and he had to put a stop to his plan of becoming a cabbie. He needed money immediately. Instead, I'd have to go it alone.

Nights were spent in front of my giant map. Days were spent on my moped, driving all over London. I navigated the roads of Hackney and Bethnal Green where I'd spent so much of my youth, past the flat above the fire station by Bow Flyover, the flat in Thornhill Square, St. Monica's boxing club, the bridge.

The Bridge.

Archway Bridge.

Suicide Bridge.

I'd try not to think about what had gone before as I whizzed past. Blocked it out. Until one day it just made no sense. The past was the past. I touched my brakes and drew the moped to a stop. I parked it in the exact same spot that I'd dumped my bicycle all those years ago. I retraced the same steps I'd taken all those years ago, my legs no longer insured for £1 million but still shaking slightly with nerves. Everything felt surreal. I reached out and touched the fence, just as I had before. I jumped onto the bridge, just as I had before. The metal was cold, just like before. I peered over the edge, saw the gold numbers, the dull red background, the cars zooming past. Just as I had before.

I stayed there for minutes that felt like hours. I looked and looked. And then I turned and jumped. Back onto the ground. Walking back towards my moped, ready to continue learning my routes. I couldn't help it. A great big smile broke across my face, running from ear to ear. My life couldn't have changed any more for the better. From the lowest of lows to my new reality: a family, friends, a new trade that I was good at, happiness, ambitions of buying a house and passing the Knowledge. It felt so unexplainably good. Blissful. As if I'd beaten something that had plagued me for years. I allowed myself a few minutes, then I readjusted the map on the front handlebars of my moped so it was nice and clear and sped off, eager to continue learning.

They say it takes two-and-a-half years of full-time study or four-and-a-half years of part-time study to complete the Knowledge. You need to learn each of the Blue Book runs: 320 runs over four books comprising 60,000 streets, being able to memorise any business or landmark on each of them, of which there are around 100,000. Sat-navs aren't allowed, which is why it's often referred to as the hardest test in the world. There have even been studies done on London cabbies that show them to have a larger posterior hippocampus – the area of the brain responsible for memory – than most people. That was part of the attraction. I wanted to be self-employed, but I also wanted to show those around me that I could do it.

From early on I knew I'd found something I was good at. Names stuck. I was getting more of my routes right than wrong. I passed the written test then flew through my first set of points, going through a series of routes with examiners and telling them how to get from Point A to Point B as directly as possible. These tests came every 56 days and every success gave me three points. Once I accumulated 12 points, I made it to the next stage, known as 28s. I was getting a proper kick out of the Knowledge. My whole life revolved around it. Even when we went on holiday I'd take my books with me to study on the beach. It used to drive Rosie nuts.

The 28s proved to be no worries and then I was on to the penultimate stage, the 21s. I was close. Every three weeks I was seeing an examiner for another set of tests. Everything had almost paid off. I'd just need to pass another three tests and then it was on to the final stage – the suburbs – which was widely considered a formality.

Then disaster struck. I was labouring down in Brixton

at Loughborough Junction, fixing a window on a council estate, when the phone call came. It was Rosie. She was hysterical. I'd never known her to be in such a state. I could barely understand her but what I could make out made my blood run cold.

"Dad's died."

I dropped the phone in shock. The whole world around me stopped. All I could hear were Rosie's tears still coming through my phone on the floor.

"I'm coming!" I screamed as I picked the phone back up in a rush. I left the site and jumped onto my moped, knowing I needed all of the routes I'd learned for the Knowledge to come good now. I had to get home as fast as possible.

As I made my way over Waterloo Bridge and down to Woburn Square, the emotions of it all hit me until it all became too much. The geezer was my idol. He meant everything to me. And now he was gone. I pulled over, tears streaming down my face, and called Mum. She was in bits, too. "I can't believe it," she repeated. He'd died of a heart attack, she told me. One second he was sitting on his bed and putting on his socks; the next he was dead. It was unexpected, totally out of the blue.

His body was still there when I arrived. Rosie remained hysterical and I wasn't feeling much better, though I tried not to show it. "Be strong," I told her, "I'm here for you," all the while wanting to keel over and cry my heart out. There were people everywhere in the room, all of them in tears. Keith was a good man who'd touched so many people's lives in ways he could never have imagined. "Thanks for helping me," I whispered to his lifeless body. "Thanks for letting me watch you and learn from you."

Six months later I passed the Knowledge. It had taken me just over three years. For the final six months I had jacked in my day job and focused everything on passing the test. It was worth it. I had my licence. I was a cabbie.

The London Taxi & Private Hire Division of Transport for London (LTPH) gave me my official badge and scorecard to confirm I had passed the Knowledge. The first thing I did was take them both to Keith's grave. I stood over the earth and thanked him once more, then stuck the scorecard into the soil.

"That one's for you, mate," I smiled.

My mission of putting together a deposit for a house was well underway. I took to life in the cab, driving into London all week, evenings, Saturdays and Sundays, and having all sorts of people get in the back of the taxi. It was a social way of life, a chance to interact with people I'd never usually. Rosie had taken on much of her dad's work with the horses and was also caring for Freya. Together, we also opened up a children's clothing shop called Pink and Blues. The money was coming along.

After my first two years in the cab we found out that our second child was on the way. We were thrilled. This time round we decided to wait until the birth to discover the gender. It seemed to be a foregone conclusion though. I had two older sisters and Rosie was one of two older sisters to a younger brother, Jack. We'd have another girl and then have a boy on the third attempt, just like both of our parents had done. This time around Rosie had a C-section. Because of her broken back, a recurring injury from horse riding, she had to have a general anaesthetic and then give birth in the operating theatre. I waited outside, listening anxiously for the first sound of life.

The moment came.

The nurse put her head round the door and asked what I thought. I could hear the cries. I already knew.

"That's definitely a girl," I said. I didn't care what it was as long as it was healthy.

"No, it's a boy."

I was in total shock.

A boy! A boy! She's only gone and done it. We've got a boy!

When Rosie came round she couldn't believe it was a boy either. All of the drugs in her system had put her completely out of it. I was telling her for about two hours. Eventually, the message went in.

Our family was complete. I'd never known happiness like it. As I sat there with our baby boy, Beau, in my arms I promised him I'd do everything I could to give him the best life possible. I would learn from the mistakes of my own father. I'd let him and Freya do whatever they pleased, guiding them rather than telling them. I'd let them have a childhood. I'd support them in whatever they did.

"You're going to have a good life," I said out loud. "You're going to have a settled life, a normal life. I'll learn from the mistakes. I'll do everything I can."

25: Finding

We were married on 19 December 2014. A winter wonderland themed wedding with Christmas trees and festive decorations on Rosie's family's land. It was the same place her parents had been married, which meant all the more after Keith's passing. We bought our first family home. Everything was perfect. I'd achieved my mission and had a beautiful wife and two beautiful children to show for it. We were happy and settled. Not even the news that a man called Greg Dyke had been made chairman of the Football Association could change my mood.

I was no longer angered by football. I'd made peace with the sport. If it was on then I'd watch it or read about it but I wouldn't go out of my way to see a game. The past was the past. I wanted to live in the present and plan for the future.

Spending time in my own house made me so proud. I wanted to be there as much as possible, tucked away with my little family. We moved in just after my 31st birthday. We painted it all up, decorated it and received sofas and furniture from friends and family. It looked brilliant. Why would I have ever wanted to be anywhere else?

New Year's Eve came around and, rather than spending

it with my mates, I wanted to be at home with my family. The BBC's coverage was enough for both of us. As we sat watching it, an idea came into my head. A mission. I always need a mission. And as the idea evolved, I realised I'd found my new mission.

"I'm going to write a book. About my life. It'll become a film."

Rosie looked at me as if she'd seen an alien. I'd told her all about my old life and my footballing exploits by this point but she still thought it was a mad idea.

"What are you talking about?" she asked.

Her reaction didn't matter. I had my new mission.

The mission gathered momentum quicker than I ever could have imagined. A few weeks into the new year I was training down the local boxing gym in Cheshunt when journalist Steve Bunce came in to do a piece. Whatever it was he intended to do, it soon got sidetracked because he clocked me and recognised me instantly. After introducing himself he asked if he could film me doing some shadow work and then interview me afterwards. Following that, he asked if we could continue the interview at Enfield playing fields.

On the drive over we carried on chatting. I told Steve all about my more recent life and my new desire to write a book.

"You know what," Steve said. "I'm going to help you."

And he did.

Later that week, I received a call from a producer who worked for the Colin Murray show on TalkSport. They were due to have Stuart Pearce and Mike Tindall in the studio and wanted me along to talk all about my career.

It had barely been six weeks since my book idea when I walked into the TalkSport studio at Hatfields in London. As soon as I entered the main office, people were greeting me.

"Hello Sonny, do you remember me? I came round your house 15 years ago."

Colin Murray came out to introduce himself. He'd spoken to Steve Bunce, he said, who'd told him all about my story. He knew he needed time. "Let's do 45 minutes and go from there," he suggested before guiding me into the studio. I sat down in between Stuart Pearce and Mike Tindall. Mike greeted me, then I turned to Stuart and said: "Nice to meet you." I couldn't believe it: Stuart Pearce! A true legend, synonymous with passion and the Three Lions.

"How are you, son?" he replied.

Colin started the interview on air by asking if my name was really Sonny. That helped settle the nerves. The interview was the first I'd done in well over a decade, and back then I was just a kid who let my dad or Terry speak for me. "Your Wikipedia page doesn't even have your date of birth," Colin added. I put him right on both accounts.

"September 12, 1983, so when I was six years old I was watching Pearcy having a right go at the World Cup." I said it without remembering Stuart Pearce's fateful penalty miss in the semi-final against Germany and got a bit of a sideways glance. I was referring to his passion for his country, though. I loved it.

Colin moved straight on, asking when I first realised I had

talent and how my career developed. I told him all about the East Anglia representative side and playing alongside Ashley Young and David Bentley, finishing the mini World Cup as top scorer with 28 goals in six games. I told of all the things that happened after that: Ajax, my legs insured for £1 million, Mizuno, Paul Smith, Coca Cola, McDonald's, the Sky Sports awards, the newspapers and the magazines and the TV shows.

"So how did it all unravel?" Colin asked. With that question I could feel the ears of the hundreds of thousands of listeners pricking up. This was the juicy part, what they really wanted to know. Just what did happen to that Sonny Pike kid?

"The attention I was getting was all positive and my dad got a bit carried away with all the money, the clothes and he was doing things he shouldn't have been doing. He got together with a journalist for a programme called *Coaching and Poaching* when I was at Orient and they videoed it, and it all blew up pretty much. They banned me for a year and I couldn't play for anyone of a decent standard. As I think about it now it's crazy, you can't get your head around it, I struggle to understand what happened.

"Parents would stand on the side of the pitch screaming 'break his legs, they're worth a million'. I never minded because I was better than everyone else but I was obsessed with football and what happened ruined me in that way."

Stuart suggested I should go into professional clubs and talk about this.

"I'd like kids to listen and learn," I responded. "I was the only one in the same situation back then and now it's non-stop. I'd love to offer some advice, about having agents at the right time and not getting carried away with that kind of thing. Let the player get a YTS, and after that you've got half a foot in the door. I was doing that at 11 and 12 but by 14 I was more or less finished.

"It's not nice to talk about. My kids haven't got a grandad because of what happened. My dad got massively carried away, he earned a lot of money. I was told he could have got £100,000 from McDonald's and the newspaper articles. It's a terrible thing. I see it from a different way now. I was looking at my kids today and saying, 'How could you do that?' Mentally, by the time I was 16, 17, I was in bits. I was finished."

"Do you possess forgiveness?" Colin asked.

"I'm a positive man now. It is what it is. It is hard to have no one to talk to about that side of the thing."

"So the circus packed up and moved out of town?"

"A lot of people went missing. Agents went missing. There are some good and bad but why does a kid need an agent when they are that young? It doesn't make sense to me. I didn't want to play football no more. The attention. The abuse. I was in a bad way for a while. There was a time when I wasn't interested in doing anything, let alone playing football."

"We've got a situation in England where Gascoigne was plying his trade and the game might have missed out on another Gascoigne," Stuart replied. "That saddens me deeply."

"It went from the beautiful game to the curse," Colin added. "You realise you've been taken for a ride and didn't want to play football anymore."

"I had to try and learn to understand what had gone on with certain things like the articles and the publicity. I went training at Palace the day after one big piece appeared in the News of the World and it was 'see you later'. The clubs didn't want to know."

"You were always being sold to the highest bidder?"

"That documentary about players being poached. I was gutted. I wanted to play for Chelsea. I want to speak to some of the people who followed through with a documentary that was negative towards the game, about poaching players, when they knew it was going to have an effect on me."

"When did you get your life back?"

"I've been on a mission since my kids were born. That started to get the circle turning. I've flipped the script and gone the other way. I'd never push my kids into doing things they didn't want to do. To parents I'd say, 'Don't get too carried away. Let the kid go to the clubs, they know what they're doing.' It's very easy for kids to be burned out. When I was 14, I was a professional. Free clothes. Money. But when it came to doing the goods, I was finished."

A weight had lifted from my shoulders. Everything that had been repressed came out and went live on national radio.

The response was incredible. As I stepped out of the studio, TalkSport employees rushed up to congratulate me. It brought back all of the memories of what my life had been like at the height of my fame. I spoke to everyone and then walked out, feeling as if I was walking on air all the way back to my taxi. There, I sat and just let the experience wash over me. I breathed in deeply, taking in the moment, relief flooding through me. After a few minutes I checked my phone and saw it'd been buzzing about like mad. There were messages from all over the place. I'd even managed to get more than 1,000 new followers on Twitter despite never posting a tweet.

Colin rang me up later that evening to say what a great interview it'd been. My name had gone viral, he reckoned. I was so clueless when it came to social media I didn't really even know what that meant, and I even had to ask Colin what a direct message on Twitter was.

It was just as well I found out, because all kinds of people were messaging me after the TalkSport interview. The book process began within days, but there were also some less welcoming ones.

'I've got a car lot in north-west London,' read one. 'Can you come outside my place and do some kick-ups. I'll get some photos of you to use as promotional material.'

Mate, no. I'm done.

As far as endorsements were concerned, I wasn't interested. There were a few areas I was looking to explore, though. Stuart's recommendation about going to professional clubs to share my experiences really struck a chord, and I was also keen to do anything for the mental health and wellbeing of young footballers. After all, I was in a position to be selective.

Goal.com took me back to Ajax for a piece of content. I went with Rosie, my mate Murray and his other half, Christine. That didn't half bring back the memories. The idea was to find Tom Pronk but unfortunately we discovered that he'd recently passed away. Instead, *Goal.com* filmed as I showed Rosie the stadium and the training ground and retraced my footsteps. It was nice to share it with her, even though she doesn't have a clue about football.

I was slowly opening up again to football. My trust was rebuilding. With everything off my plate, I felt more free. People began asking me for my opinion on football. I found myself going out of my way to watch games on TV. 'What's going on here?' I thought. The more questions I was asked, the more intrigued I got. Before I knew it I was looking at team kits and scrolling through all of the new boot designs, just like I used to when I was a kid. I'd go to my local shop and see all these multi-coloured boots and those with sock support and be full of wonder. Boots had come a long way since those gold Mizunos that I had.

And then I had to buy a pair of boots for myself. Colin Murray called up to invite me to play in a charity game in Wales against semi-pro side Pontypridd Town. He was putting together a TalkSport team and wondered if I wanted in.

I said 'yes' in a heartbeat.

I bought myself a pair of black adidas Copa Mundials. The feelings all came back. There was plenty of excitement about wearing my new boots for the first time. Quality. As it was my first game in well over a decade I didn't think I'd need two pairs, so I went with moulded studs. That was a big mistake. When we got to Wales we found torrential rain. The pitch was sodden, totally the wrong weather for moulded studs. If the game wasn't for charity then was no way it'd have been played.

There were a lot of decent ex-pros in our team. Danny Murphy, Phil Babb, Matt Holland, Dietmar Hamann, Matthew Etherington, Danny Gabbidon, Perry Groves, Simon Davies. Still, I got the nod to start up top.

Mum and Terry came along to watch from the stands. As I lined up it felt just like before. Football felt just like before. The pressure was gone. The paranoia deserted me. I just wanted to have fun. And not be blowing out of my arse after 10 minutes.

Fitness was a concern. I'd done a few runs in preparation but nothing as intense as a game of 90 minutes. I knew my touch would still be there but was unsure how long I'd last.

I got to half-time and felt I'd done well. I'd held the ball up and helped stuff to happen around me. As expected, Pontypridd were more organised than us but we'd given as good as we'd got. "He's staying on," Danny Murphy announced as we sat around the small changing rooms at half-time, pointing in my direction. An ex-Liverpool player, impressed by my performance! Half of me was buzzing at a little recognition, especially when it was met with agreement by our team-mates, but the other half was screaming, 'I'm knackered already.'

Colin was my get-out. I knew he wanted a game and so at 80 minutes, with my legs run into the ground, I called over to the bench and asked for a change. Colin took my place up front; I took Colin's place behind the mic.

We lost 3-1 but the day proved a success, so much so that Colin got me involved in another charity game, this time in benefit of non-league club Chester FC. Colin got some big names involved for his 'all-star' team to take on a Chester FC Select XI. Michael Owen, Jason McAteer and Ian Rush were all there in the changing room as I arrived clutching on to my Copa Mundials. Talk about legends! I thought back to those countless days in the playground where I'd pretended to be Ian Rush and couldn't help but smile. I asked him for a photo straight away and he obliged. He was as good as gold. We lost 4-1 but were all smiles after another quality evening.

The bug was back. I'd fallen in love with football once more. At times I even thought about finding a team and getting a proper pre-season under my belt. But then the realities of life struck. Kids, mortgage, work, family.

I still felt there was something there for me in football, though. That was part of the beauty of self-employment as a cabbie. I could do what I wanted, when I wanted. And hadn't Ajax said I had the potential to be a decent coach all those years ago? As the bug continued to bite, I found myself giving greater consideration to those words from all those years ago. It ticked all the boxes. I could help others, focus on their mental health and also ensure they could play the game to the best of their ability.

"I'll feel wasted if I don't do something," I told Rosie. "I'm enjoying football."

"Do what you gotta do," she replied.

I went into a few clubs and talked about my experiences. I spoke at a conference in the Corinthia Hotel, London. Then I went up to Leeds to speak at the university there. I was with the students all day but didn't give my presentation until the very end. Until then, they'd been looking at me wondering who I was. I stood up on stage and announced myself.

"Look, I'm Sonny Pike. When I was a kid I was meant to be the next big thing but it didn't work out. I didn't know how to deal with it, things didn't go right and I felt a lot of pressure." I looked out at the audience and saw they'd gone from wondering who I was to their eyes popping, locked in as if they knew. I was shocked that they were engaged. After speaking for 15 minutes I asked for questions, not really expecting any, only to have loads of hands raised.

I came out of that lecture hall walking on clouds. It felt like I'd really helped the students. It felt good.

I wanted that feeling again.

Years earlier, I'd done a bit of coaching for a mate of Adam's, someone called Andy Russell. It had involved after-school clubs and holiday camps. It was enjoyable but not right for me at a time when I wanted to be out with my mates as much as possible, when playing the game was still raw. This time felt different though. More tempting. And so I booked myself onto an FA Coaching Badge course. Following that, I spent hours trawling the internet and seeing what was going on. I didn't fancy coaching at a club or managing a team. What I really wanted to do was coach young players in the same way I was coached. My own little thing, teaching my own little values in the game: close control, technique, skill. One-on-one coaching kept on coming up. Social media was brilliant for finding examples of sessions and seeing what else people were doing out there.

"I could do that," I pointed out to Rosie.

"Go on then. Why don't you just train kids then?"

I dipped my toe in the water and set up pages on Facebook and Instagram for Sonny Pike 1 on 1 Coaching. My first player soon got in touch and I arranged to do a session later that week with him on Enfield Playing Fields. It made sense to start my coaching journey at the same place I'd started my football journey with Enfield Colts. It made sense, that is, until I arrived to give the session. I got there half-an-hour early, a little nervous. But when I pulled in I found the barriers to the car park up. That was odd. I'd never seen the car park shut before. After parking around the corner and walking onto the fields, I saw why. There were tens of caravans all over the fields. Travellers had settled and the council had obviously put in measures to dissuade more joining. Typical. Bloody typical. My first-ever coaching session and I was going to have to do it around the caravans! It was too late to find anywhere else. I sent a text message to the parents of the player, telling them to park up around the corner.

It can't have looked the most professional set-up when the player arrived. I greeted him and then put him into action, throwing everything into my coaching to try and make up for the chaos all around us. We started off with ladder work to get his feet moving and his energy up, then it was onto the exact drills I was brought up on: passing, lots of touches, skills. There were also a couple of exercises from Ajax thrown in, such as the above-head clapping while dribbling.

I must have done something right because the player came back. And he wasn't the only one. More players contacted me. Before long I was struggling to find spaces to fit them in, especially if I still went into London in my taxi. I packed as many players into the long summer days as I could. As the days shortened, though, the realisation dawned that I couldn't keep training on public parks. I'd need a place with floodlights, where I could train kids outside of school and cab-driving hours.

"Rosie, I've got so many kids I can't fit them in. If I want to do this I need to do if properly," I told her late one night.

"Look, do what you got to do," she replied. "You're a nightmare when you get something into your head, so just get on and do it."

Together, we agreed to speak to Rosie's mum, who had plenty of space at the yard. We found that she was very much open to helping me out. She let me have one of the fields in her plot by the M25 and said I could do what I wanted to with it.

I'd got something into my head and I was about to get it out.

Over the next four months I set about building my field of dreams. The Sonny Pike 1 on 1 Academy would be an indoor facility of turf that allowed for practice at any hour. It'd be big enough for two v two, wide enough to fit a goal in for shooting practice, small enough to keep sessions intimate. If ever things needed to change, there was plenty of the field left. I could always stick floodlights on it and brave the cold.

Plenty of favours were called in. Mates of Rosie's family built the foundations. Gary did all the electrics at a ridiculously cheap price. A gym session with Adam at Lee Valley – Bucky's employer – got us the astroturf when Adam spotted it about to be thrown out. A deal with the owner seemed brilliant until the turf was laid. It looked fine, but I didn't want my academy to be fine. I wanted it to be perfect. A new turf was laid, and then the final touches: the goal, the equipment, the quotes from Johan Cruyff and Ronaldo on the wall.

Talent without hard work is nothing.

Football has to be fun for kids or it doesn't make sense.

The positive impact of football is obvious as I go about my sessions. I've never been in a better place with the sport. Players have come to me and gained confidence, become more outgoing, improved their game and felt more stable in everything they do. Training together has helped players achieve their goals – whether that's to push on into an academy or simply to become more confident – allowed them to forget their problems and given them hours of fun and enjoyment. That's all that I can ask of the sport.

At the end of the day, that's exactly what football should be about. Kids should enjoy playing the game and feel free to express themselves with the ball. Football is a simple game, made complicated by adults.

When I played football, before everything fell apart, I felt completely free. It didn't matter where I was or what I was going through, everything was lost in the game. That's exactly how it should be.

There's more to life than football.

There's more to my life than football.

But what football can do to life is undoubtable.

26: The Next Big Thing

"Here, Sonny. Can you coach my kid mate?"

"Who is he?"

"Well, my boy is five. He's not a normal five-year-old though."

"Oh right."

"No. He swims three times a week. He's got a personal trainer coming in twice a week and he also does golf. Now I want to get him started on football."

Are you for real?

It turned out the geezer on the other end of the phone line was absolutely for real. I told him to bring his kid along. I was ready to educate him.

People have coined my career as 'Sonny Pike syndrome' and applied it to other promising young talents. In situations where players are hyped up by the media with increasing pressure – not helped by the increasing commercialisation of football, development of social media and arrival of the influencer generation – the burden of expectation weighs heavy. Ten-year-old kids with hundreds of thousands of social media followers front advertising campaigns for the biggest sportswear manufacturers. Clips of six-year-olds doing skills go viral, with viewers commenting the kid is destined for big things. Parents continue to push, seeing sport as a valid pathway to untold riches.

That five-year-old boy's dad? There'll be thousands of people like him around the country. Yet how many talented young players will ever make it? According to Mike Calvin, author of *No Hunger in Paradise*, only 180 of the 1.5 million players who are playing organised youth football in England at any one time will ever play as a Premier League pro.

It's easy for parents to get carried away. Clubs scout players so young now that it's possible for five-year-olds to be representing the biggest teams in the country. The stakes have never been higher. Or so it'd seem.

Not all parents will know how football works. Many will be like my dad was. When that's the case, the parents need to get as much advice as they can from those around them. They need to learn from other people's experiences. Assess where their kid is at. Preach the value of hard work without ever forcing them into something. Let their talent grow as naturally as possible. Allow them to experience the process without putting too much pressure on them. A challenge is healthy, but never expect them to do something they can't do.

Doing anything to an elite level can be a lonely task as a young person. While others lead normal lives and go for sleepovers, cinema visits and parties, they must train and meet club, county and even international commitments –

all while keeping up with their school work. Burnout is a risk. Mental health must be monitored.

Looking back on my story has lifted a weight from my shoulders. As I write this, I consider myself as happy as can be. Would I have changed my past to just lead a normal life and avoid the spotlight? Absolutely. But I have no regrets about what happened. Right now, as a cabbie and football coach with a loving family, I consider myself to be in the best position possible. I'm stable, normal, happy. All of those negatives I experienced at such a young age allowed me to learn a lot about life and embrace the positives.

When I learned to accept myself for what I was, I found life became much more manageable. Back when it all went wrong, I thought that being well known would give me an easier ride in whatever I did. Making friends, getting work, labouring, finding a new club. It never quite happened. Yet when I accepted the fact I was a labourer, I flipped that belief. I realised that because of my past I'd have to work harder than anyone else. It gave me a fire, a motivation to push myself. The positive of being 'well known' became a negative, which then became a positive.

Terry always used to tell me about 'the mirror'. "Everyone's got a mirror to come home to," he'd say. It took me a long time to work out what he meant. Those who wrong you, who cause you pain and suffering, have to go and look at themselves in the mirror. They have to live with what they've done. That can provide comfort. Agents have to live with their manipulation. Those who used me for their own personal gain are stuck with what they've done. At the same time, you also have to go and look at yourself in the mirror. It's a chance to strip everything back and be brutally honest. Are you doing enough? Are you being lazy? What do you see looking back at you? You have to be completely honest. It doesn't always have to be negative. When I was beating myself up for being unable to change the FA's decision and overturn my ban from football, all I could see was a useless kid. But what I should have seen was a nice kid, a good person, a kid who was still a talented footballer. It took me a while to learn how to use the mirror. When I was doing the Knowledge, I'd look in the mirror and be kinder to myself. I'd think, 'You know what, you're doing well here.' It was a chance to congratulate myself. No matter what you see in the mirror, though, you have to be accountable. Once you start blaming others, you're on a slippery slope. Take responsibility, work out how to change the person you see in the mirror for the better, then go out and do that.

There's no growth in comfort. Everyone can challenge themselves to do better. But at the same time, they shouldn't get consumed by one thing. My life as a kid was football, football, football. Football was my identity. When that got taken away, it was devastating. Side missions are healthy. They provide perspective, give you time to rest and engage your brain in other ways. It could be learning a new language or reading a book. Each side mission completed is then a small win, and lots of small wins combined equal one great win.

Life is hard. Football is hard. Things are going to happen and, at times, that will be upsetting. Dreams will be broken, realities will be exploited. People will be chewed up and spat out. But that doesn't mean we all can't still achieve.

It took me until the age of 14 to learn to say 'no'.

It might take the five-year-old even longer to say 'no'. If it does then that's a whole decade of structured, relentless training that they're going to go through, maybe even more. A whole childhood missed.

Education can change that.

Focusing on mental health can change that.

Allowing young people to express themselves will change that.

Making sure young people enjoy themselves will change that.

Putting them at the front and centre, always being aware of their feelings, their motivations, their dreams, will change that.

And maybe then, once and for all, we'll overcome Sonny Pike syndrome.

27: In Dad's Defence

FACEBOOK MESSENGER NOTIFICATION.
MESSAGE REQUEST FROM MICKEY PIKE.
ACTIVE NOW:

'Here is some information you may require for the book I'm told you are writing.

The TV bloke contacted me one day, saying that he had seen you and heard about your talents, and could he follow and film me in your day-to-day routine at home, training, etc.

There wasn't a mention of the programme that Dyke was going to make and, at this point, I had never even seen Dyke.

[The cameraman] filmed you in the gym and over the park. He did say that he would like to take you to the training camp of the England Under-21 squad, and the footage that he would take we could have as a keepsake.

This went on and off for a few weeks. He was gaining my confidence. He knew that you were at Orient and asked if he could come along. I asked Barry Hearn if that was okay. If you remember, we had a meeting with Barry Hearn in his office and he gave you a full kit. Permission was given from him, thinking it would be a nice film about you and the Orient.

Just by chance, a Chelsea scout rang me at that time asking what you were up to and would you like to go to their youth training camp. I told [the cameraman] this and he said that he would like to come and film you. This would be just for his own property and not to be used on TV. He would also give us a copy.

I rang the Youth FA, asking if I could take you there as you were at the Orient. They said they would get back to me but never did.

[He] said that it was just for a training session and they wouldn't mind. As you know, I don't know anything about football and I knew you'd have wanted to go, so along we went on a Thursday evening.

[He] had a small camera which he used to film with. I didn't realise that he was doing it covertly in the shadows to make the whole thing look shady.

They then filmed you on the pitch at the Orient ground and [he] said he'd send us a copy of the film that he had made.

THAT WAS THE LAST I SAW OF HIM.

The next thing I knew was me and you were sitting in Grandad and Nanny's caravan on Sheppy one Sunday morning when we saw the headline from The News Of The World: 'Chelsea tried to steal my son.'

I never even spoke to any writer, let alone say that rubbish.

That was a statement put out by the TV company for the documentary about youth football coming out called *Fair Game*, which you were the main feature of.

When we found out the date of its TV release, your then coach Terry Welch asked Mum (not me) if he could put on a do in his local pub. He wanted to throw a little party for you with his mates when it aired. I wasn't asked for my opinion.

I didn't show up that night to watch it with you because I didn't want you shown off in a pub like a freak. My sights were higher, so I stayed at home and watched the first half then walked out with the hump.

We had been used and had been made fools of. I knew that you would feel the backlash from it.

I tried to get Greg Dyke on the phone but he hid behind his secretary and the like.

Mum used this to split us even more, saying I took money and everything. (I'm not saying this to run your mum down, I'm just saying it how it was. The past is the past.)

I was mad for a long while after that and, if I could have got my hands on Dyke, I would have chinned him.

Well, you know what happened after that. They made Chelsea look bad and me a user of you.

And after that we got even further apart.

YOU DON'T NEED TO REPLY SONNY BUT IF YOU HAVE ANY QUESTIONS YOU CAN ASK.

TAKE CARE,

DAD.'

If you reply, Mickey will be able to call you and see information such as your Active Status and when you've read messages.

I didn't reply.

28: The Pikes

We were sitting in the Fish & Eels pub, near Broxbourne, when Terry told us the news. He had cancer. Lung cancer. Me and Rosie looked at each other, the long summer day drawing to a close, then looked at Terry, both of us in absolute shock. The man with the heart of gold who had fought so many battles for me looked as if he was fighting his final battle. Later that night, we agreed that Terry didn't look as if he'd make it to Christmas.

For days, I was absolutely gutted. Totally shocked. I resolved to do everything I could for him. It was time to pay Terry back for all of the stuff he'd done for me. He'd come round regularly anyway, but from the diagnosis we started seeing him every week. He loved coming over and playing with the dog and hearing how Freya and Beau were getting on, and we loved seeing him.

That was six years ago now.

Terry's still going.

He's been in and out of hospitals but continues to be winning his fight against cancer. The mindset of that man is like nothing I've ever seen before. He might only be small in stature but his determination is infectious. He will not be beaten. He will still do the things he loves. Even at the age of 84 he's off down the golf course to play a round when the weather is good.

Joey came out of prison after eight long years. Over that time, Joe had moved all over the country, from HMP Belmarsh to Chelmsford, High Point in Newmarket, Full Sutton in York, Whitemoor in Cambridgeshire. Never in the same place for longer than two years, shifting to more lenient prisons as he was deemed less of a threat. Throughout that time I continued visiting him. Rosie often accompanied me on the long drives, even staying overnight in a hotel when he was up in York. The two of us would check up on him and see he was doing okay. He was also helping the other prisoners by working as a Samaritans listener. We chatted away and then, as soon as we were back, in the car we would play *Locked Up* by Akon on full volume, trying our best to readjust to normal life.

I met him on the day that he became a free man. We went over to Mum's house in Wormley and sat round trading stories with the kettle on. As I told him all about what I'd been doing, Joey stopped me mid-sentence.

"Son, in this time, what you've done…You've left me behind."

"Don't say that."

"You have. Look at you. You're up and down, off to work every day, trying to get stuff going. You've got a lovely family. You're making things happen."

Bloody hell.

A lot has changed. I used to see Joey as a big man who had

everything. Over the years, that had reversed. Now Joey saw me as the person with everything. It was his way of saying he was proud.

Joey faded out of our lives. It was time for a fresh start. He got himself involved in property.

Dad remains out of my life. We haven't spoken a word to each other since that fateful day with Terry when he said he didn't have a son. Over the years, my feelings have softened. He got carried away, I can see that. He wanted me to become a star. That was always the dream. It wasn't necessarily for me to play for England or for me to make him millions. He wanted me to be everywhere. In doing so, he surrounded us with the wrong kind of people, got the wrong kind of idea and ended up damaging everything more than he ever could have known.

Though I haven't seen him since that day, Rosie bumped into him while heavily pregnant with Freya.

"You can go in front of me," Dad smiled at her in the queue to pay for petrol. "You're fatter than me." Rosie looked like she'd seen a ghost. She knew exactly who he was; he didn't have a clue that he was speaking to his daughter-in-law. Since then, Dad has sent occasional messages to me through Rosie on Facebook. He asks after Freya and Beau, and tells Rosie to let me know that he loves me. The last I heard, he lived on a caravan site. In the days of wining and dining agents and mixing with the stars at the Sky Sports awards, he never could have imagined that this is how it would turn out.

Freya and Beau are starting to do their own thing. Freya

has taken after her mum and gotten into horses. The two of them are always off down the yard to tend to them. More recently, Freya started competing in showjumping with a four-day event in Wales.

"You're not going to believe this," Rosie told me in the car as we drove along the M4. "But the sidelines won't be too different to what they're like in football." Leave it out, I told her. You can't be serious. When I got there, I realised she was being deadly serious. The horses all wait outside to be called into the arena. There must have been up to 40 of them, all with different kinds of riders. There was a lot of money floating about, some of the horses worth upwards of £30,000, many of them with top-class riders, but Freya more than held her own. As other riders got grilled something rotten by their parents for messing up their round, we watched on with tears in our eyes. That was our girl out there. Rosie was blubbing before Freya had even gone over a jump. "Leave it out!" I told her. On the final day, though, cor, it tore me up. Only qualifying riders are invited back for the final day of the event and Freya made the cut. As she hung in there amongst the rest of the competitors on top-class ponies, tears rolled down my cheeks. In her first-ever competition she finished fifth.

She's gone on to compete in plenty more shows. Terry comes along to the events held in the yard. The two of us head up into the café, grab a cup of tea and watch on from above. Terry can't help himself, he talks as if he knows what is going on and even tries to give coaching advice to Freya on showjumping. He used to work with horses in the army, to be fair, though I'm not sure he ever took any of them showjumping.

His advice to Beau is more welcome. It was never my particular intention to get Beau into football. It was always my plan to take a back seat and let him find his own interests. Just as Freya has followed her mum into horses, however, Beau has followed me into football. I often have to do a double take as I hear from our back garden the same words I heard from all those years ago. "A steady head is the golden thread that runs through the game of football," Terry says as he shows Beau the correct technique for shooting at goal. "Know your stuff, never bluff."

It was Beau's cousins on Rosie's side of the family, Albert and Teddy, who got him into football. Albert older than him, Teddy the same age, went down to training sessions at Wormley every Saturday. As soon as Beau found out, he was on at me and Rosie to take him down as well.

For a few seconds, I wondered if it was the right thing to do. Football had caused me so much pain, been so cruel to me. I wanted to protect my son. But then I remembered all of those joyful times in Aldersbrook Park and thought it'd be wrong to deny him that. Beau could make his own decisions, find out what he enjoyed and what he didn't. Do what he wanted to. And it helped that Wormley's football ground backed onto Mum's front garden.

The next Saturday, we decided to give it a go. Beau took to the pitch alongside his older cousins and came off absolutely buzzing. He loved his experience and couldn't wait to do it all over again.

Every Saturday from then onwards I took Beau to Wormley, watched him for an hour, and then took him to Mum's house, where she'd make me a cup of tea and Beau a pancake or whatever else he wanted. She likes the company and the arrangement suits all of us. Mum's often out and about but she always values family time.

Dad's actions provide a stark warning for me when it comes to Beau. There are positives that I can take from him: the mindset, the get-up-and-go attitude, the desire to remain an individual. Most important, though, are the warning signs from which I suffered and that remind me I can't get carried away, that I need to let Beau do what he enjoys and put no pressure on him. It's working so far. Beau loves football. It's becoming just as much a part of his life as it was mine. He's always kicking balls about in the house. If he sees a skill in a game on TV, he'll try and copy it in the living room. He hasn't yet broken any of our lights or vases but he's caused havoc with Rosie's scented candles. When he isn't kicking about in the house, he's up in his room playing FIFA. He stands at the foot of his bed, face two inches from the screen as he follows the action. I have to go in there regularly to move him back and get him to put his glasses on. Often, he'll challenge me to a game. At first I could beat him but now I don't stand a chance. He knows all of the buttons and tactics and tells me what to do. Up in that room, he's surrounded by all of his heroes. Football posters line the walls. There's Mohamed Salah, Sadio Mane, James Maddison, Eden Hazard. Like me at that age with my Cruyff and Maradona and Pele videos, he tends to support players rather than teams. If pushed, he'll tell you he supports Liverpool. That's if I'm in the room, however, because the team he supports changes every five minutes! In just the last year he's supported Liverpool, Tottenham, Manchester City and Arsenal. He loves them all. He loves football.

As he fell further in love with the game and counted the days until every Wormley session, me and Rosie realised he needed to get more of his fix. We'd been planning to buy Terry tickets to a Manchester United game for Christmas – why not take Beau along as well?

On Christmas Day we gave Terry an envelope containing his tickets for the Tottenham v Manchester United game at Wembley the following month. I've rarely seen that man show emotion but I could see tears starting to well up, which made me start to well up. I had to excuse myself as he thanked us all. He hadn't been to Wembley since the '80s, he said when we settled down for dinner. He'd always been a big United fan. For the thousandth time, he reminisced about the Busby Babes and Duncan Edwards and for the thousandth time we all listened in.

Three weeks later, Rosie dropped me, Terry and Beau right at the entrance to Wembley. Terry's health wasn't at its best and we were worried about getting him in and out of the stadium but he took it all in his stride. "What the hell is going on here?" he wondered as we made our way up the escalators to our seats. "They didn't have all this the last time I came." Beau was in just as much wonder. A proper game of football! At Wembley! I just smiled at the sight of both of them: one starting his love affair with football, the other with a lifetime of football behind him, both in awe. Terry watched on in joy as Marcus Rashford gave United a 1-0 win, his only blip coming when he saw the price they were charging for fish and chips in the stadium. Beau watched the whole game, never once becoming bored or distracted, then raced around the stadium at the full-time whistle. He was so excited and couldn't wait to tell all his mates about it.

Even that didn't satisfy Beau's football fix. We took him to more games, then took him to more football sessions. He started at an Elite Feet after-school club on Monday afternoons when he was in reception at Goffs Oak primary, and from there got invited along to pre-academy sessions with a professional club.

I talked everything over with Rosie. I was still unsure about putting Beau into an elite environment. Would I be able to overcome the same downfalls that my dad suffered? Would I be able to support him? For several nights our talks remained the same. Should we? Shouldn't we?

In the end, we decided it was the right thing to do. We'd let him try it for himself and put no pressure on him. If he's happy to do it, he can do it. If he's not happy, he doesn't have to. We'd give him the comfort to settle in at one club and enjoy himself there, rather than moving all over the place like I'd been made to do.

As Beau warmed up for his first pre-academy session, the coaches all introduced themselves to me. I said "hello" and then we got onto the subject of the other coaches at the club.

"There's this guy called Bucky who does the 16s. Honestly, he's the best coach we've have ever had. He's unbelievable."

I couldn't believe my ears. I hadn't even told them that I knew Bucky and here they were, saying all of these things about the kid I used to play knock down ginger with. The kid who I sat alongside on the swings at the park and played flick-shoe with, seeing who could launch their shoe the furthest. The kid I sat down with when *London Tonight* filmed us. The young adult who did everything he could to help me achieve my dream.

And then Bucky was there, standing next to me on the sidelines after finishing his training session with the under-16s.

"Cor, this is weird isn't it?" he commented. Weird? Not half. "He's the exact replica of you at that age, isn't he?" Bucky pointed at Beau, running around in his kit, his long curly hair bouncing up and down. "Well, other than the fact he tackles and kicks people as well as doing all the skills," Bucky laughed.

Everything could have worked out so differently for me. Not that I think about that anymore. As I stand at the stables watching Freya riding her pony, as I stand on the sidelines watching Beau trying the skills that he practises in front of the TV, surrounded by Mum and Rosie and Terry and our extended families, I don't think about what could have been.

I think about everything that I have.

And I feel so lucky.

Acknowledgements

Firstly, this book may not have been possible without the help of Steve Bunce. Steve helped to get my story started by getting me onto the Colin Murray Show on TalkSport.

Both Steve and Colin have been there for me whenever I've needed any advice and have been a great help throughout.

When I met Seth Burkett for the first time we talked through different options for my book. We would meet in a coffee shop and drink green tea together and I never once felt pushed into doing anything. It was just like speaking to a friend. Looking back over messages, emails and random WhatsApp voice notes, I've sent him things on weekends and late at nights and he has always just got on with it (nothing is a problem). From start to finish, Seth has been first-class.

Reach Sport: For me, finding the right publisher was very important, and these guys have shared my passion to make my story about football and mental health. Will Beedles, Paul Dove and all of the team have been brilliant in coming up with ideas and plans to help my story keep growing. I thank them for being very professional and for all of their hard work. I couldn't have asked for better publishers.

I can simply say Terry Welch has been a lot more than a football coach. He has always been there for me through hard times and has never asked me for anything in return. His mental strength has been the biggest gift I could ever have from him. He is a real life Mickey (from Rocky the movie). We need as many Terrys in this world as possible.

I would like to say thank you to my good friends, Ben Collins, Adam 'Hitman', Gary Carter, Arran Hall, Roy Cowley and Murray and Christine Hammond. You were always there for me. Sometimes we take friends for granted but with you that's never been the case.

Sadly, Keith Hockley, Rosie's dad, suddenly passed away in 2012. Keith was someone I loved to listen to. He wasn't just a great businessman, but a real character. He was always up for a laugh, and he would go to the end of the world and back for his family. His desire to help his kids is quite simply unmatched. Joanne Hockley has helped me whenever I've needed it. She's even given me the opportunity to build my own Football Academy thanks to her generous donation of land, which is greatly appreciated.

Mum has been there for me in every situation, good or bad, never once leaving my side. My sisters Victoria and Dominique have also been through all of this with me – and been through lots themselves. This book is about me, but very much about them, too. Hopefully, this will put all of the past to bed and signal a fresh start for all of us. In looking back, I can at least say that the harder it got, the closer we became as a family. The same goes for my extended family. My uncle Victor and his family have also always been there if needed.

Rosie, my wife, has put up with me at my worst and has always been there to support me over the last 14 years. She deserves credit for this as much as I do because if it wasn't for her, to be honest, I'm not sure where I would be now. She is a brilliant mum and a lovely person.

And as for my kids: FREYA & BEAU, THIS BOOK IS FOR YOU!

mercury spor
Dream comes true for 11-year-old Sonny Pike
Ajax trial for Cheshunt's star in the making
SONNY PIKE
SOCCER PRODIGY WINS AWARD
Fill your boots
Lawrence Donegan on the cut-throat trade in young footballers
just want to play football, simple as that
Sonn Dutc Aja
up
NEWS FOCUS
Salmo
Rec star Sonny with Dutch gia
Soccer sta shoots for
Young ace has trials with top European club
By Simon Jones
HE'S currently the hottest prospect in British football.
Pet Bu
Man or m
Unhappy
Staggeri
INDOWS by porchways
OW THE TCH DO IT
Too early to play to win
The boy split up
Parents go to court in battle over their soccer prodigy son
femail ON SUNDAY
whose talent a family
Johan Cruyff: Ajax nurtured the star from an early age
Sonny Pike: The British youngster was invited to train with the club's youth team
Ajax every kid was en a ball to play with
EUROPEAN Subbuteo CHAMPIONSHIPS
AUTOGRAPHS
McDonald's